One hundred words for equality

A glossary of terms on equality between women and men

Employment & social affairs

Equal opportunities and family policy

European Commission
Directorate-General for Employment, Industrial Relations
and Social Affairs
Unit V/D.5

Manuscript completed in January 1998

Acknowledgements

The European Commission unit in charge of equal opportunities would like to express its gratitude to colleag
in other services and experts in Member States consulted for their assistance in the production of this gloss
The gratitude extends particularly to the European Commission Translation Service in Luxembourg for its c
mitment and involvement.

The contents of this publication do not necessarily reflect the opinion or position of the European Commiss
Directorate-General for Employment, Industrial Relations and Social Affairs.

A great deal of additional information on the European Union is available on the Internet.
It can be accessed through the Europa server (http://europa.eu.int).

Cataloguing data can be found at the end of this publication.

Luxembourg: Office for Official Publications of the European Communities, 1998

ISBN 92-828-2627-9

Printed in Germany

PRINTED ON WHITE CHLORINE-FREE PAPER

oreword

nce the very beginning, the European Union has played a significant role in the promotion of equality
tween women and men. In recent years, through four consecutive mid-term action programmes for equal
pportunities and through legislation where necessary, we have developed this role and intensified our
tion.

ost recently, the signature of the Treaty of Amsterdam has given a fresh impetus as it not only explicitly
cludes equality between women and men among the Community priority objectives but also states that,
all its activities, the Community shall aim at eliminating inequalities and promoting equality between
omen and men.

is glossary is part of that impetus. It is the first attempt to put together all the terms commonly used in
e area of equality policy, and it will go some way towards creating a common language in Europe for all
tors in this field.

ee the glossary as serving two extremely important objectives. First, by creating a common understanding
terms and issues at the European level, it will facilitate the promotion of equality between women and
en as foreseen by the Amsterdam Treaty. Second, and no less important, it will serve the Community con-
rn of getting the information about European policies out of the circle of initiated people and making it
cessible and understandable to all citizens. The glossary will bring our work in this area closer to the citi-
n, by clarifying the terms we use and thereby, making what we do easier to understand.

ese are worthy objectives.

elieve that the glossary will prove itself to be an invaluable tool and point of reference. It is addressed to
licy-makers, to Members of Parliament, both at the national and European level, to those working in the
d, to those simply interested, and to all women and men.

uality is a question of democracy and fundamental rights; it is a matter for us all. I commend this glossary
you.

Pádraig Flynn
*Member of the European
Commission with responsibility
for employment and social affairs*

Contents

A

B

C

D

E

5

A

ACTIVITY RATE

ES:	TASA DE ACTIVIDAD	FR:	TAUX D'ACTIVITÉ
DA:	ERHVERVSFREKVENS	IT:	TASSO DI ATTIVITÀ
DE:	ERWERBSQUOTE	NL:	ARBEIDSDEELNAME / PARTICIPATIEGRAAD
EL:	ΠΟΣΟΣΤΟ ΣΥΜΜΕΤΟΧΗΣ ΣΤΟΝ	PT:	TAXA DE ACTIVIDADE
	ΟΙΚΟΝΟΜΙΚΑ ΕΝΕΡΓΟ ΠΛΗΘΥΣΜΟ	FI:	TYÖSSÄKÄYNTIASTE
EN:	ACTIVITY RATE	SV:	FÖRVÄRVSFREKVENS

Represents the labour force as a percentage of the population of working age (15 to 64).

AFFIRMATIVE ACTION

ES:	ACCIÓN POSITIVA	IT:	AZIONI POSITIVE
DA:	POSITIV SÆRBEHANDLING	NL:	POSITIEVE ACTIE/POSITIEVE DISCRIMINATIE
DE:	FÖRDERMASSNAHMEN	PT:	ACÇÃO POSITIVA
EL:	ΘΕΤΙΚΗ ΔΡΑΣΗ	FI:	POSITIIVISET ERITYISTOIMET
EN:	AFFIRMATIVE ACTION	SV:	AKTIVA ÅTGÄRDER
FR:	ACTION POSITIVE		

See 'Positive action'.

ASSISTING SPOUSES

ES:	CÓNYUGES COLABORADORES	FR:	CONJOINTS AIDANTS/COLLABORATEURS
DA:	MEDHJÆLPENDE ÆGTEFÆLLE	IT:	COADIUVANTI
DE:	MITHELFENDE EHEGATTINNEN/	NL:	MEEWERKENDE ECHTGENOTEN
	EHEGATTEN	PT:	CÔNJUGES COLABORADORES
EL:	ΣΥΜΒΟΗΘΟΥΝΤΕΣ ΣΥΖΥΓΟΙ	FI:	AVUSTAVAT PUOLISOT
EN:	ASSISTING SPOUSES	SV:	MEDHJÄLPANDE MAKAR

The spouses of people who are engaged in work usually of a self-employed or independent nature, where the spouse is an important contributor to the work but does not necessarily receive direct remuneration for this work and is often not entitled to social protection benefits.

ATYPICAL WORK/EMPLOYMENT

ES: EMPLEO O TRABAJO ATÍPICO

DA: ATYPISK ARBEJDE

DE: ATYPISCHE ARBEIT/
BESCHÄFTIGUNGSVERHÄLTNISSE

EL: ΑΤΥΠΗ ΕΡΓΑΣΙΑ/ΑΠΑΣΧΟΛΗΣΗ

EN: ATYPICAL WORK/EMPLOYMENT

FR: TRAVAIL/EMPLOI ATYPIQUE

IT: LAVORO ATIPICO

NL: FLEXIBELE ARBEID

PT: EMPREGO/TRABALHO ATÍPICO

FI: EPÄTYYPILLINEN TYÖ

SV: ATYPISKT ARBETE

Work other than full-time and permanent work, including part-time, evening and weekend work, fixed-term work, temporary or subcontract home-based work, telework and outwork.

BALANCED PARTICIPATION OF WOMEN AND MEN

S:	PARTICIPACIÓN EQUILIBRADA DE MUJERES Y HOMBRES
A:	JÆVN KØNSFORDELING
E:	AUSGEWOGENE MITWIRKUNG VON FRAUEN UND MÄNNERN
L:	ΙΣΟΡΡΟΠΗ ΣΥΜΜΕΤΟΧΗ ΓΥΝΑΙΚΩΝ ΚΑΙ ΑΝΔΡΩΝ
N:	BALANCED PARTICIPATION OF WOMEN AND MEN
R:	PARTICIPATION ÉQUILIBRÉE DES FEMMES ET DES HOMMES

IT:	PARTECIPAZIONE EQUILIBRATA DI DONNE E UOMINI
NL:	EVENWICHTIGE DEELNAME VAN MANNEN EN VROUWEN
PT:	PARTICIPAÇÃO EQUILIBRADA DE MULHERES E HOMENS
FI:	NAISTEN JA MIESTEN TASAPUOLINEN OSALLISTUMINEN
SV:	JÄMN FÖRDELNING MELLAN KVINNOR OCH MÄN

The sharing of power and decision-making positions (40 to 60 % representation of either sex) between men and women in every sphere of life, which constitutes an important condition for equality between men and women Council Recommendation 96/694/EC of 2 December 1996, OJ L 319, 10.12.1996).

BENCHMARKING

S:	EVALUACIÓN COMPARATIVA
A:	»BENCHMARKING«
E:	„BENCHMARKING"
L:	ΟΡΟΣΗΜΑΝΣΗ ΤΩΝ ΕΠΙΔΟΣΕΩΝ
N:	BENCHMARKING
R:	ÉTALONNAGE DES PERFORMANCES

IT:	ANALISI COMPARATIVA DELLE PRESTAZIONI
NL:	IJKING
PT:	AVALIAÇÃO/ANÁLISE COMPARATIVA
FI:	ESIKUVA-ANALYYSI
SV:	BENCHMARKING

The establishment of a criterion, standard or reference point against which o establish targets and measure progress.

B

ES:	CARGA DE LA PRUEBA	IT:	ONERE DELLA PROVA
DA:	BEVISBYRDE	NL:	BEWIJSLAST
DE:	BEWEISLAST	PT:	ÓNUS DA PROVA
EL:	ΒΑΡΟΣ ΑΠΟΔΕΙΞΗΣ	FI:	TODISTUSTAAKKA
EN:	BURDEN OF PROOF	SV:	BEVISBÖRDA
FR:	CHARGE DE LA PREUVE		

If a person files a legal complaint, it is in principle up to him or her to prove that he or she has been a victim of discrimination. In the area of equal treatment between men and women, a directive, based on the case-law of the Court of Justice of the European Communities, shifts the burden of proof between the parties (defendant and complainant). Where persons consider themselves wronged by failure to apply the principle of equal treatment and where there is a prima facie case of discrimination, it is for the respondent to prove that there has been no contravention of the principle (judgment of 17 October 1989, Case C 109/88 *Danfoss* [1989] ECR 3199, paragraph 16; Council directive of 15 December 1997 on the burden of proof in cases of discrimination based on sex).

C

CHILDCARE

S:	ATENCIÓN A LA INFANCIA	IT:	CUSTODIA DEI BAMBINI
DA:	BØRNEPASNING	NL:	KINDEROPVANG
DE:	KINDERBETREUUNG	PT:	ACOLHIMENTO DE CRIANÇAS
L:	ΦΡΟΝΤΙΔΑ ΠΑΙΔΙΩΝ	FI:	LASTENHOITO
EN:	CHILDCARE	SV:	BARNOMSORG
FR:	GARDE D'ENFANTS		

A broadly based concept covering the provision of public, private, individual or collective services to meet the needs of children and parents (Council Recommendation 92/241/EEC of 31 March 1992, OJ L 123, 8.5.1992).

D

DEMOCRATIC DEFICIT

ES:	DÉFICIT DEMOCRÁTICO	IT:	DEFICIT DEMOCRATICO
DA:	DEMOKRATISK UNDERSKUD	NL:	DEMOCRATISCH TEKORT
DE:	DEMOKRATIEDEFIZIT	PT:	DÉFICE DEMOCRÁTICO
EL:	ΔΗΜΟΚΡΑΤΙΚΟ ΕΛΛΕΙΜΜΑ	FI:	DEMOKRATIAVAJE
EN:	DEMOCRATIC DEFICIT	SV:	DEMOKRATISKT UNDERSKOTT
FR:	DÉFICIT DÉMOCRATIQUE		

The impact of, for example, inadequate gender balance on the legitimacy of democracy.

DEPENDANT CARE

ES:	ATENCIÓN A PERSONAS DEPENDIENTES	IT:	ASSISTENZA ALLE PERSONE NON AUTONOME
DA:	OMSORG (eller pleje)	NL:	VERZORGING VAN AFHANKELIJKE PERSONEN
DE:	BETREUUNG ABHÄNGIGER	PT:	CUIDADOS A PESSOAS DEPENDENTES
EL:	ΦΡΟΝΤΙΔΑ ΕΞΑΡΤΩΜΕΝΩΝ ΑΤΟΜΩΝ	FI:	OMAISHOITO
EN:	DEPENDANT CARE	SV:	VÅRD AV NÄRSTÅENDE
FR:	SOINS AUX PERSONNES DÉPENDANTES		

Provision of care for those who are young, ill, elderly or disabled and dependent on another.

DERIVED RIGHTS

ES:	DERECHOS DERIVADOS	IT:	DIRITTI DERIVATI
DA:	AFLEDTE RETTIGHEDER	NL:	AFGELEIDE RECHTEN
DE:	ABGELEITETE ANSPRÜCHE/RECHTE	PT:	DIREITOS DERIVADOS
EL:	ΕΛΚΟΜΕΝΑ ΔΙΚΑΙΩΜΑΤΑ	FI:	JOHDETUT OIKEUDET
EN:	DERIVED RIGHTS	SV:	HÄRLEDDA RÄTTIGHETER
FR:	DROITS DÉRIVÉS		

Rights, notably to social security benefits or residence, which accrue to an individual but which originate from and depend on his or her relationship with another person, usually of parenthood, marriage or cohabitation.

DESEGREGATION OF THE LABOUR MARKET

ES:	DESEGREGACIÓN DEL MERCADO DE TRABAJO	IT:	DISGREGAZIONE DEL MERCATO DEL LAVORO
DA:	AFSKAFFELSE AF KØNSOPDELINGEN PÅ	NL:	DESEGREGATIE VAN DE ARBEIDSMARKT
	ARBEJDSMARKEDET	PT:	DESSEGREGAÇÃO DO MERCADO
DE:	ABBAU DER TEILUNG DES ARBEITSMARKTES		DE TRABALHO
EL:	ΕΞΑΛΕΙΨΗ ΤΩΝ ΔΙΑΧΩΡΙΣΜΩΝ ΣΤΗΝ	FI:	TYÖMARKKINOIDEN ERIYTYMISEN
	ΑΓΟΡΑ ΕΡΓΑΣΙΑΣ		VÄHENTÄMINEN
EN:	DESEGREGATION OF THE LABOUR MARKET	SV:	DESEGREGERING AV ARBETSMARKNADEN
FR:	DÉSÉGRÉGATION DU MARCHÉ DU TRAVAIL		

Policies aiming to reduce or eliminate segregation (vertical/horizontal) in the labour market.

DIGNITY AT WORK

ES:	DIGNIDAD EN EL TRABAJO	IT:	DIGNITÀ SUL LAVORO
DA:	VÆRDIGHED PÅ ARBEJDSPLADSEN	NL:	WAARDIGHEID OP HET WERK
DE:	WÜRDE AM ARBEITSPLATZ	PT:	DIGNIDADE NO TRABALHO
EL:	ΑΞΙΟΠΡΕΠΕΙΑ ΣΤΟ ΧΩΡΟ ΕΡΓΑΣΙΑΣ	FI:	IHMISARVOINEN KOHTELU TYÖPAIKOILLA
EN:	DIGNITY AT WORK	SV:	VÄRDIGHET PÅ ARBETSPLATSEN
FR:	DIGNITÉ AU TRAVAIL		

The right to respect and, in particular, freedom from sexual and other forms of harassment in the workplace (Council Resolution 90/C 157/02 of 29 May 1990, OJ C 157, 27.6.1990).

D

ES: DIRECTIVAS SOBRE LA IGUALDAD DE TRATO
DA: DIREKTIVER OM LIGEBEHANDLING
DE: GLEICHBEHANDLUNGSRICHTLINIEN
EL: ΟΔΗΓΙΕΣ ΠΟΥ ΑΦΟΡΟΥΝ ΤΗΝ ΙΣΗ
     ΜΕΤΑΧΕΙΡΙΣΗ
EN: DIRECTIVES ON EQUAL TREATMENT
FR: DIRECTIVES SUR L'ÉGALITÉ DE TRAITEMENT

IT: DIRETTIVE SULLA PARITÀ DI TRATTAMENTO
NL: RICHTLIJNEN INZAKE GELIJKE BEHANDELING
PT: DIRECTIVAS SOBRE A IGUALDADE
     DE TRATAMENTO
FI: TASA-ARVOISTA KOHTELUA KOSKEVAT
     DIREKTIIVIT
SV: DIREKTIV OM LIKA BEHANDLING

Directives which extend the scope of the principle of equal treatment fo
men and women (which initially, in the Treaty of Rome, only concernec
pay). The principle was extended to access to employment, vocational train
ing and promotion, and working conditions (Council Directive 76/207/EEC o
9 February 1976, OJ L 39, 14.2.1976), to statutory social security scheme:
(Council Directive 79/7/EEC of 19 December 1978, OJ L 6, 10.1.1979), to occu
pational social security schemes (Council Directive 86/378/EEC of 24 July
1986, OJ L 225, 12.8.1986), to those engaged in activity, including in agri
culture, in a self-employed capacity (Council Directive 86/613/EEC of 1'
December 1986, OJ L 359, 19.12.1986), to pregnant workers and worker
who have recently given birth (Council Directive 92/85/EEC of 19 Octobe
1992, OJ L 348, 28.11.1992) and to those who are on parental leave (Counci
Directive 96/34/EC of 3 June 1996, OJ L 145, 19.6.1996).

ES: DIVERSIDAD
DA: FORSKELLIGHED
DE: UNTERSCHIEDLICHKEIT
EL: ΠΟΙΚΙΛΟΜΟΡΦΙΑ
EN: DIVERSITY
FR: DIVERSITÉ

IT: DIVERSITÀ
NL: DIVERSITEIT
PT: DIVERSIDADE
FI: MONIMUOTOISUUS
SV: MÅNGFALD

The range of values, attitudes, cultural perspective, beliefs, ethnic back
ground, sexual orientation, skills, knowledge and life experiences of th
individuals making up any given group of people.

DIVISION OF LABOUR (by gender)

S:	DIVISIÓN DEL TRABAJO (debida al género)	FR:	DIVISION DU TRAVAIL (selon le sexe)
DA:	ARBEJDSDELING EFTER KØN	IT:	DIVISIONE DEL LAVORO (per sesso)
DE:	(geschlechtsspezifische) ARBEITSTEILUNG	NL:	ARBEIDSVERDELING (naar geslacht)
EL:	ΚΑΤΑΜΕΡΙΣΜΟΣ ΤΗΣ ΕΡΓΑΣΙΑΣ	PT:	DIVISÃO DO TRABALHO (por género)
	(κατά φύλο)	FI:	SUKUPUOLTEN VÄLINEN TYÖNJAKO
EN:	DIVISION OF LABOUR (by gender)	SV:	ARBETSFÖRDELNING (efter kön)

The division of paid and unpaid work between women and men in private and public life.

DOMESTIC VIOLENCE/FAMILY VIOLENCE

S:	VIOLENCIA DOMÉSTICA/VIOLENCIA EN LA FAMILIA	FR:	VIOLENCE DOMESTIQUE/DANS LA FAMILLE
DA:	VOLD I HJEMMET/FAMILIEN	IT:	VIOLENZA IN AMBITO DOMESTICO/FAMILIARE
DE:	HÄUSLICHE GEWALT/GEWALT IN DER FAMILIE	NL:	HUISELIJK GEWELD/GEWELD BINNEN HET GEZIN
EL:	ΒΙΑ ΜΕΣΑ ΣΤΟ ΣΠΙΤΙ/ΒΙΑ ΜΕΣΑ ΣΤΗΝ ΟΙΚΟΓΕΝΕΙΑ	PT:	VIOLÊNCIA DOMÉSTICA/NA FAMÍLIA
		FI:	PERHEVÄKIVALTA
EN:	DOMESTIC VIOLENCE/FAMILY VIOLENCE	SV:	VÅLD I HEMMET/VÅLD INOM FAMILJEN

Any form of physical, sexual or psychological violence which puts the safety or welfare of a family member at risk and/or the use of physical or emotional force or threat of physical force, including sexual violence, within the family or household. Includes child abuse, incest, wife battering and sexual or other abuse of any member of the household.

E

ECONOMICALLY ACTIVE POPULATION

ES:	POBLACIÓN ACTIVA	FR:	POPULATION ACTIVE
DA:	DEN ØKONOMISK AKTIVE BEFOLKNING	IT:	POPOLAZIONE ATTIVA
DE:	ERWERBSBEVÖLKERUNG/	NL:	ECONOMISCH ACTIEVE BEVOLKING
	ERWERBSPERSONEN	PT:	POPULAÇÃO ECONOMICAMENTE ACTIVA
EL:	OIKONOMIKA ΕΝΕΡΓΟΣ ΠΛΗΘΥΣΜΟΣ	FI:	TYÖVOIMA
EN:	ECONOMICALLY ACTIVE POPULATION	SV:	FÖRVÄRVSARBETANDE BEFOLKNING

All persons of either sex who supply labour for the production of economi
goods and services as defined by the UN (United Nations) system of nation
al accounts during a specified time period.

EMPOWERMENT

ES:	CAPACITACIÓN (para una plena	EN:	EMPOWERMENT
	participación en los procesos	FR:	RENFORCEMENT DE POUVOIR
	de toma de decisiones)	IT:	CONFERIMENTO DI RESPONSABILITÀ
DA:	SÆTTEN I STAND TIL AT DELTAGE	NL:	„EMPOWERMENT"
	I SAMFUNDET PÅ LIGE FOD	PT:	CAPACITAÇÃO
DE:	„EMPOWERMENT"	FI:	VAIKUTUSVALLAN LISÄÄMINEN
EL:	ΕΝΔΥΝΑΜΩΣΗ	SV:	ÖKAD DELAKTIGHET

The process of gaining access to resources and developing one's capacitie
with a view to participating actively in shaping one's own life and that o
one's community in economic, social and political terms.

EQUALITY BETWEEN WOMEN AND MEN (sex equality)

ES:	IGUALDAD ENTRE MUJERES Y HOMBRES	FR:	ÉGALITÉ ENTRE LES FEMMES ET LES HOMME
	(igualdad entre los sexos)		(égalité des sexes)
DA:	LIGESTILLING MELLEM KVINDER	IT:	PARITÀ TRA DONNE E UOMINI
	OG MÆND (kønsligestilling)		(parità tra i sessi)
DE:	GLEICHSTELLUNG VON FRAUEN UND	NL:	GELIJKHEID VAN VROUWEN EN MANNEN
	MÄNNERN (Gleichstellung der Geschlechter)	PT:	IGUALDADE ENTRE MULHERES E HOMENS
EL:	ΙΣΟΤΗΤΑ ΜΕΤΑΞΥ ΓΥΝΑΙΚΩΝ ΚΑΙ ΑΝΔΡΩΝ		(igualdade entre os sexos)
	(ισότητα των φύλων)	FI:	NAISTEN JA MIESTEN VÄLINEN TASA-ARVO
EN:	EQUALITY BETWEEN WOMEN AND MEN	SV:	JÄMSTÄLLDHET MELLAN KVINNOR
	(sex equality)		OCH MÄN

The principle of equal rights and equal treatment for women and men (se
'Gender equality').

EQUALITY DIMENSION

S:	DIMENSIÓN DE LA IGUALDAD	IT:	DIMENSIONE DI PARITÀ
DA:	LIGESTILLINGSDIMENSION	NL:	GELIJKHEIDSDIMENSIE/
DE:	GLEICHSTELLUNGSDIMENSION		EMANCIPATIEASPECTEN
EL:	ΔΙΑΣΤΑΣΗ ΤΗΣ ΙΣΟΤΗΤΑΣ	PT:	DIMENSÃO DA IGUALDADE
EN:	EQUALITY DIMENSION	FI:	TASA-ARVOULOTTUVUUS
FR:	DIMENSION DE L'ÉGALITÉ	SV:	JÄMSTÄLLDHETSASPEKT

The aspect of any issue which relates to equality.

EQUAL OPPORTUNITIES FOR WOMEN AND MEN

ES:	IGUALDAD DE OPORTUNIDADES	IT:	PARI OPPORTUNITÀ PER DONNE E UOMINI
	ENTRE MUJERES Y HOMBRES	NL:	GELIJKE KANSEN VOOR
DA:	LIGE MULIGHEDER FOR KVINDER OG MÆND		VROUWEN EN MANNEN
DE:	CHANCENGLEICHHEIT	PT:	IGUALDADE DE OPORTUNIDADES
	FÜR FRAUEN UND MÄNNER		ENTRE MULHERES E HOMENS
EL:	ΙΣΕΣ ΕΥΚΑΙΡΙΕΣ ΓΙΑ ΓΥΝΑΙΚΕΣ ΚΑΙ ΑΝΔΡΕΣ	FI:	NAISTEN JA MIESTEN TASA-ARVOISET
EN:	EQUAL OPPORTUNITIES FOR WOMEN AND MEN		MAHDOLLISUUDET
FR:	ÉGALITÉ DES CHANCES ENTRE	SV:	LIKA MÖJLIGHETER FÖR KVINNOR OCH MÄN
	LES FEMMES ET LES HOMMES		

The absence of barriers to economic, political and social participation on the grounds of sex.

EQUAL PAY FOR WORK OF EQUAL VALUE

ES:	IGUALDAD DE RETRIBUCIÓN POR	IT:	PARITÀ DI RETRIBUZIONE PER LAVORO
	UN TRABAJO DE IGUAL VALOR		DI PARI VALORE ,
DA:	LIGE LØN FOR ARBEJDE AF SAMME VÆRDI	NL:	GELIJK LOON VOOR ARBEID
DE:	GLEICHES ENTGELT BEI		VAN GELIJKE WAARDE
	GLEICHWERTIGER ARBEIT	PT:	IGUALDADE DE REMUNERAÇÃO
EL:	ΙΣΗ ΑΜΟΙΒΗ ΓΙΑ ΕΡΓΑΣΙΑ ΙΣΗΣ ΑΞΙΑΣ		POR TRABALHO DE IGUAL VALOR
EN:	EQUAL PAY FOR WORK OF EQUAL VALUE	FI:	SAMA PALKKA SAMANARVOISESTA TYÖSTÄ
FR:	RÉMUNÉRATION ÉGALE POUR TRAVAIL	SV:	LIKA LÖN FÖR LIKVÄRDIGT ARBETE
	DE VALEUR ÉGALE		

Equal pay for work to which equal value is attributed without discrimination on grounds of sex or marital status with regard to all aspects of pay and conditions of remuneration (Article 141 (ex 119) of the Amsterdam Treaty).

E

ES: IGUALDAD DE TRATO ENTRE
MUJERES Y HOMBRES

DA: LIGEBEHANDLING AF KVINDER OG MÆND

DE: GLEICHBEHANDLUNG VON FRAUEN
UND MÄNNERN

EL: ΙΣΗ ΜΕΤΑΧΕΙΡΙΣΗ ΓΥΝΑΙΚΩΝ ΚΑΙ ΑΝΔΡΩΝ

EN: EQUAL TREATMENT FOR WOMEN AND MEN

FR: ÉGALITÉ DE TRAITEMENT ENTRE
LES FEMMES ET LES HOMMES

IT: PARITÀ DI TRATTAMENTO PER DONNE
E UOMINI

NL: GELIJKE BEHANDELING VAN VROUWEN
EN MANNEN

PT: IGUALDADE DE TRATAMENTO
ENTRE MULHERES E HOMENS

FI: NAISTEN JA MIESTEN YHTÄLÄINEN KOHTELU

SV: LIKA BEHANDLING AV KVINNOR OCH MÄN

Ensuring the absence of discrimination on the grounds of sex, either directly or indirectly (see 'Sex discrimination').

F

FAMILY LEAVE

ES:	PERMISO POR RAZONES FAMILIARES	IT:	CONGEDO PER MOTIVI FAMILIARI
DA:	ORLOV AF FAMILIEMÆSSIGE ÅRSAGER	NL:	VERLOF WEGENS FAMILIEOMSTANDIGHEDEN
DE:	URLAUB AUS FAMILIÄREN GRÜNDEN	PT:	LICENÇA PARA ASSISTÊNCIA À FAMÍLIA
EL:	ΑΔΕΙΑ ΓΙΑ ΟΙΚΟΓΕΝΕΙΑΚΟΥΣ ΛΟΓΟΥΣ	FI:	PERHEVAPAA
EN:	FAMILY LEAVE	SV:	LEDIGHET AV FAMILJESKÄL
FR:	CONGÉS POUR RAISONS FAMILIALES		

A right to leave for family reasons which may or may not be shared between the parents.

FAMILY VIOLENCE

ES:	VIOLENCIA EN LA FAMILIA	IT:	VIOLENZA NEL CONTESTO FAMILIARE
DA:	VOLD I FAMILIEN	NL:	GEWELD BINNEN HET GEZIN
DE:	GEWALT IN DER FAMILIE	PT:	VIOLÊNCIA NA FAMÍLIA
EL:	ΒΙΑ ΜΕΣΑ ΣΤΗΝ ΟΙΚΟΓΕΝΕΙΑ	FI:	PERHEVÄKIVALTA
EN:	FAMILY VIOLENCE	SV:	VÅLD INOM FAMILJEN
FR:	VIOLENCE DANS LA FAMILLE		

See 'Domestic violence'.

FAMILY WORKER

ES:	AYUDA FAMILIAR	FR:	AIDE FAMILIALE
DA:	MEDHJÆLPENDE FAMILIEMEDLEM	IT:	COLLABORATORE NELL'IMPRESA FAMILIARE
DE:	MITHELFENDE FAMILIENANGEHÖRIGE	NL:	MEEWERKEND GEZINSLID
EL:	ΕΡΓΑΖΟΜΕΝΟΣ/Η ΣΤΗΝ ΟΙΚΟΓΕΝΕΙΑΚΗ	PT:	TRABALHADOR FAMILIAR
	ΕΠΙΧΕΙΡΗΣΗ	FI:	PERHEYRITYKSESSÄ TYÖSKENTELEVÄ
EN:	FAMILY WORKER	SV:	MEDHJÄLPANDE FAMILJEMEDLEM

A family member working in a family business such as a farm, shop, small business or professional practice; frequently a wife, daughter or son.

FEMINISATION OF POVERTY

ES: FEMINIZACIÓN DE LA POBREZA
DA: FEMINISERING AF FATTIGDOMMEN
DE: FEMINISIERUNG DER ARMUT
EL: ΑΥΞΗΣΗ ΤΟΥ ΠΟΣΟΣΤΟΥ ΤΩΝ ΓΥΝΑΙΚΩΝ
ΜΕΤΑΞΥ ΤΩΝ ΦΤΩΧΩΝ
EN: FEMINISATION OF POVERTY

FR: FÉMINISATION DE LA PAUVRETÉ
IT: FEMMINILIZZAZIONE DELLA POVERTÀ
NL: FEMINISERING VAN DE ARMOEDE
PT: FEMINIZAÇÃO DA POBREZA
FI: KÖYHYYDEN NAISISTUMINEN
SV: FEMINISERING AV FATTIGDOMEN

The increasing incidence and prevalence of poverty among women as compared with men.

FLEXIBILITY OF WORKING TIME/WORKING HOURS

ES: HORARIO FLEXIBLE
DA: FLEKSIBEL ARBEJDSTID
DE: FLEXIBLE ARBEITSZEIT
EL: ΕΥΕΛΙΞΙΑ ΤΟΥ ΧΡΟΝΟΥ/ΤΩΝ
ΩΡΩΝ ΕΡΓΑΣΙΑ
EN: FLEXIBILITY OF WORKING TIME/
WORKING HOURS

FR: FLEXIBILITÉ DU TEMPS/DES HORAIRES
DE TRAVAIL
IT: FLESSIBILITÀ DELL'ORARIO DI LAVORO
NL: FLEXIBELE ARBEIDSDUUR/WERKTIJDEN
PT: FLEXIBILIDADE DO TEMPO DE TRABALHO/
/HORÁRIO DE TRABALHO
FI: TYÖAIKAJOUSTO / JOUSTAVA TYÖAIKA
SV: FLEXIBEL ARBETSTID

Formulas of working time which offer a range of possibilities in relation to the number of hours worked and the arrangements of rosters, shifts or work schedules on a daily, weekly, monthly or yearly basis.

G

GENDER

ES:	GÉNERO/SEXO, TOMADO EN SENTIDO SOCIOLÓGICO	FR:	GENRE/SEXE (rapports sociaux de sexe)
DA:	KØN	IT:	GENERE
DE:	SOZIALES GESCHLECHT	NL:	GENDER
EL:	ΦΥΛΟ (κοινωνικό)	PT:	GÉNERO
EN:	GENDER	FI:	SUKUPUOLI (GENDER)
		SV:	GENUS

A concept that refers to the social differences, as opposed to the biological ones, between women and men that have been learned, are changeable over time and have wide variations both within and between cultures.

GENDER ANALYSIS

ES:	ANÁLISIS POR GÉNERO	IT:	ANALISI COMPARATIVA DI GENERE
DA:	KØNSSPECIFIK ANALYSE	NL:	GENDERANALYSE
DE:	GESCHLECHTSSPEZIFISCHE ANALYSE	PT:	ANÁLISE DAS QUESTÕES DO GÉNERO
EL:	ΑΝΑΛΥΣΗ ΩΣ ΠΡΟΣ ΤΟ ΦΥΛΟ	FI:	TASA-ARVOANALYYSI
EN:	GENDER ANALYSIS	SV:	JÄMSTÄLLDHETSANALYS/GENUSANALYS
FR:	ANALYSE SELON LE GENRE		

The study of differences in the conditions, needs, participation rates, access to resources and development, control of assets, decision-making powers, etc., between women and men in their assigned gender roles.

GENDER AUDIT

ES:	ANÁLISIS EN FUNCIÓN DEL GÉNERO	IT:	VERIFICA DELL'INTEGRAZIONE DELLA DIMENSIONE DI GENERE
DA:	LIGESTILLINGSMÆSSIG VURDERING	NL:	GENDERAUDIT
DE:	GLEICHSTELLUNGSKONTROLLE	PT:	COMPROVAÇÃO DA INTEGRAÇÃO DA PERSPECTIVA DO GÉNERO
EL:	ΕΛΕΓΧΟΣ ΩΣ ΠΡΟΣ ΤΟ ΦΥΛΟ		
EN:	GENDER AUDIT	FI:	TASA-ARVOTARKASTUS
FR:	AUDIT SELON LE GENRE	SV:	JÄMSTÄLLDHETSREVISION

The analysis and evaluation of policies, programmes and institutions in terms of how they apply gender-related criteria.

G

ES:	VIOLENCIA SEXISTA	IT:	VIOLENZA CONNESSA AL SESSO
DA:	KØNSBASERET VOLD	NL:	SEKSUEEL GEWELD
DE:	GESCHLECHTSBEZOGENE GEWALT	PT:	VIOLÊNCIA LIGADA AO SEXO/VIOLÊNCIA
EL:	ΒΙΑ ΠΟΥ ΣΥΝΔΕΕΤΑΙ ΜΕ ΤΟ ΦΥΛΟ		SEXUAL
EN:	GENDER-BASED VIOLENCE/SEXUAL VIOLENCE	FI:	SUKUPUOLISTUNUT VÄKIVALTA
FR:	VIOLENCE LIÉE AU GENRE/SEXE	SV:	KÖNSRELATERAT VÅLD

Any form of violence by use or threat of physical or emotional force, including rape, wife battering, sexual harassment, incest and paedophilia.

ES:	INSENSIBLE A LAS DIFERENCIAS DE GÉNERO	IT:	INSENSIBILE ALLA SPECIFICITÀ DI GENERE
DA:	KØNSBLIND	NL:	GENDERBLIND
DE:	GLEICHSTELLUNGSINDIFFERENT	PT:	INSENSÍVEL À DIMENSÃO DO GÉNERO
EL:	ΑΓΝΟΩΝ/ΟΥΣΑ ΤΗ ΔΙΑΣΤΑΣΗ ΤΟΥ ΦΥΛΟΥ	FI:	SUKUPUOLISOKEA
EN:	GENDER BLIND	SV:	KÖNSBLIND
FR:	IGNORANT LA SPÉCIFICITÉ DE GENRE		

Ignoring/failing to address the gender dimension (as opposed to gender
sensitive or gender neutral).

ES:	CONTRATO BASADO	IT:	CONTRATTO SOCIALE IN BASE AL SESSO
	EN LAS DIFERENCIAS DE GÉNERO	NL:	GENDERCONTRACT/CONTRACT
DA:	KØNSKONTRAKT		TUSSEN MANNEN EN VROUWEN
DE:	GESCHLECHTERVERTRAG	PT:	CONTRATO SOCIAL DO GÉNERO
EL:	ΚΟΙΝΩΝΙΚΟ ΣΥΜΒΟΛΑΙΟ ΤΟΥ ΦΥΛΟΥ	FI:	SUKUPUOLISOPIMUS
EN:	GENDER CONTRACT	SV:	GENUSKONTRAKT
FR:	CONTRAT SOCIAL DE GENRE		

A set of implicit and explicit rules governing gender relations which allocate
different work and value, responsibilities and obligations to men and
women and maintained on three levels: cultural superstructure: the norms
and values of society; institutions — family welfare, education and employment systems, etc.; and socialisation processes, notably in the family.

GENDER DIMENSION

ES:	DIMENSIÓN DEL GÉNERO	IT:	SPECIFICITÀ DI GENERE
DA:	KØNSDIMENSION	NL:	GENDERDIMENSIE/EMANCIPATIEASPECTEN
DE:	GESCHLECHTSSPEZIFISCHE DIMENSION	PT:	DIMENSÃO DO GÉNERO
EL:	ΔΙΑΣΤΑΣΗ ΤΟΥ ΦΥΛΟΥ	FI:	SUKUPUOLIULOTTUVUUS
EN:	GENDER DIMENSION	SV:	KÖNSASPEKT/JÄMSTÄLLDHETSASPEKT
FR:	SPÉCIFICITÉ DE GENRE		

The aspect of any issue which relates to gender/the differences in the lives of women and men.

GENDER DISAGGREGATED DATA

ES:	DATOS DESAGREGADOS POR SEXO	FR:	DONNÉES VENTILÉES PAR SEXE
DA:	KØNSOPDELTE DATA	IT:	DATI DISAGGREGATI IN BASE AL SESSO
DE:	NACH GESCHLECHT AUFGESCHLÜSSELTE DATEN	NL:	NAAR GESLACHT UITGESPLITSTE GEGEVENS
		PT:	DADOS REPARTIDOS POR GÉNERO
EL:	ΔΕΔΟΜΕΝΑ ΚΑΤΑ ΦΥΛΟ	FI:	SUKUPUOLEN MUKAAN ERITELLYT TIEDOT
EN:	GENDER DISAGGREGATED DATA	SV:	KÖNSUPPDELADE UPPGIFTER

The collection and separation of data and statistical information by gender to enable comparative analysis/gender analysis.

GENDER DISTRIBUTION OF PAID AND UNPAID WORK

ES:	DISTRIBUCIÓN DEL TRABAJO REMUNERADO Y NO REMUNERADO EN FUNCIÓN DEL GÉNERO	IT:	RIPARTIZIONE DI LAVORO RETRIBUITO E NON RETRIBUITO IN BASE AL SESSO
DA:	FORDELING AF LØNNET OG ULØNNET ARBEJDE MELLEM KØNNENE	NL:	VERDELING VAN BETAALDE EN ONBETAALDE ARBEID TUSSEN MANNEN EN VROUWEN
DE:	GESCHLECHTSSPEZIFISCHE AUFTEILUNG VON BEZAHLTER UND UNBEZAHLTER ARBEIT	PT:	DISTRIBUIÇÃO POR GÉNEROS DO TRABALHO REMUNERADO E NÃO REMUNERADO EM FUNÇÃO DO GÉNERO
EL:	ΚΑΤΑΝΟΜΗ ΚΑΤΑ ΦΥΛΟ ΤΗΣ ΑΜΕΙΒΟΜΕΝΗΣ ΚΑΙ ΜΗ ΑΜΕΙΒΟΜΕΝΗΣ ΕΡΓΑΣΙΑΣ		
EN:	GENDER DISTRIBUTION OF PAID AND UNPAID WORK	FI:	PALKALLISEN JA PALKATTOMAN TYÖN JAKAUTUMINEN SUKUPUOLEN MUKAAN
FR:	RÉPARTITION DU TRAVAIL RÉMUNÉRÉ ET NON RÉMUNÉRÉ ENTRE LES FEMMES ET LES HOMMES	SV:	KÖNSFÖRDELNING NÄR DET GÄLLER AVLÖNAT OCH OAVLÖNAT ARBETE

See 'Division of labour (by gender)'.

G

ES: IGUALDAD ENTRE HOMBRES Y MUJERES
DA: LIGESTILLING MELLEM KØNNENE
DE: GLEICHSTELLUNG DER GESCHLECHTER/
   GLEICHSTELLUNG VON FRAUEN
   UND MÄNNERN (in sozialer Hinsicht)
EL: ΙΣΟΤΗΤΑ ΤΩΝ ΦΥΛΩΝ
EN: GENDER EQUALITY

FR: ÉGALITÉ DES SEXES
IT: UGUAGLIANZA TRA I SESSI
NL: GELIJKHEID VAN MANNEN EN VROUWEN
PT: IGUALDADE ENTRE GÉNEROS
FI: SUKUPUOLTEN TASA-ARVO
SV: JÄMSTÄLLDHET MELLAN KVINNOR
   OCH MÄN

The concept that all human beings are free to develop their personal abilities and make choices without the limitations set by strict gender roles; that the different behaviour, aspirations and needs of women and men are considered, valued and favoured equally.

ES: EQUIDAD ENTRE HOMBRES Y MUJERES
DA: RIMELIG BALANCE MELLEM KØNNENE
DE: GLEICHHEIT VON FRAU UND MANN
EL: ΙΣΟΤΙΜΙΑ ΤΩΝ ΦΥΛΩΝ
EN: GENDER EQUITY
FR: TRAITEMENT ÉQUITABLE ENTRE LES SEXES
IT: UGUAGLIANZA DI GENERE

NL: GELIJKWAARDIGE BEHANDELING
   VAN MANNEN EN VROUWEN
PT: EQUIDADE ENTRE GÉNEROS
FI: SUKUPUOLTEN OIKEUDENMUKAINEN
   KOHTELU
SV: LIKVÄRDIG BEHANDLING

Fairness of treatment by gender, which may be equal treatment or treatment which is different but which is considered equivalent in terms of rights, benefits, obligations and opportunities.

ES: DIFERENCIA DEBIDA AL GÉNERO
DA: KØNSSKÆVHED
DE: GESCHLECHTSSPEZIFISCHE DISKREPANZ
EL: ΑΝΟΙΓΜΑ ΜΕΤΑΞΥ ΤΩΝ ΦΥΛΩΝ
EN: GENDER GAP
FR: DISPARITÉ ENTRE LES GENRES

IT: DISPARITÀ TRA I GENERI
NL: GENDERKLOOF/VERSCHILLEN
   TUSSEN VROUWEN EN MANNEN
PT: FOSSO ENTRE GÉNEROS
FI: SUKUPUOLTEN VÄLINEN KUILU
SV: KLYFTAN MELLAN KÖNEN

The gap in any area between women and men in terms of their levels of participation, access to resources, rights, remuneration or benefits.

G

GENDER IMPACT ASSESSMENT

ES:	EVALUACIÓN DEL IMPACTO EN FUNCIÓN DEL GÉNERO	FR:	ÉVALUATION DE L'IMPACT SELON LE GENRE
DA:	KØNSSPECIFIK KONSEKVENSANALYSE	IT:	VALUTAZIONE D'IMPATTO RISPETTO AL SESSO
DE:	BEWERTUNG DER GESCHLECHTS-SPEZIFISCHEN AUSWIRKUNGEN	NL:	EMANCIPATIE-EFFECTRAPPORTAGE
EL:	ΕΚΤΙΜΗΣΗ ΤΟΥ ΑΝΤΙΚΤΥΠΟΥ	PT:	AVALIAÇÃO DO IMPACTO NO GÉNERO
	(μιας πολιτικής) ΣΤΟ ΦΥΛΟ	FI:	SUKUPUOLIVAIKUTUSTEN ARVIOINTI
EN:	GENDER IMPACT ASSESSMENT	SV:	KONSEKVENSANALYS UR ETT JÄMSTÄLLDHETS PERSPEKTIV

Examining policy proposals to see whether they will affect women and men differently, with a view to adapting these proposals to make sure that discriminatory effects are neutralised and that gender equality is promoted.

GENDER MAINSTREAMING

ES:	INTEGRACIÓN DE LA PERSPECTIVA DE GÉNERO EN EL CONJUNTO DE LAS POLÍTICAS/TRASVERSALIDAD	EN:	GENDER MAINSTREAMING
		FR:	INTÉGRATION DE LA DIMENSION DE GENRE
DA:	INTEGRERING AF KØNSASPEKTET I ALLE POLITIKKER	IT:	MAINSTREAMING (integrazione della dimensione delle pari opportunità)
DE:	„GENDER MAINSTREAMING"/EINBEZIEHUNG DER DIMENSION DER CHANCENGLEICHHEIT IN SÄMTLICHE BEREICHE DER POLITIK/ QUERSCHNITTSAUFGABE FRAUEN- UND GLEICHSTELLUNGSPOLITIK	NL:	INTEGRATIE VAN DE GENDERDIMENSIE/ EMANCIPATIEASPECTEN IN HET BELEID
		PT:	INTEGRAÇÃO DA PERSPECTIVA DO GÉNERO
		FI:	VALTAVIRTAISTAMINEN (mainstreaming)
EL:	ΕΝΤΑΞΗ ΤΗΣ ΔΙΑΣΤΑΣΗΣ ΤΟΥ ΦΥΛΟΥ	SV:	INTEGRERING AV ETT JÄMSTÄLLDHETSPERSPEKTIV

The systematic integration of the respective situations, priorities and needs of women and men in all policies and with a view to promoting equality between women and men and mobilising all general policies and measures specifically for the purpose of achieving equality by actively and openly taking into account, at the planning stage, their effects on the respective situations of women and men in implementation, monitoring and evaluation (Commission communication, COM(96) 67 final, 21.2.1996).

G

ES:	NO DISCRIMINATORIO CON RESPECTO AL SEXO/NO SEXISTA
DA:	KØNSNEUTRAL
DE:	GESCHLECHTSNEUTRAL
EL:	ΟΥΔΕΤΕΡΟΣ/Η/Ο ΩΣ ΠΡΟΣ ΤΟ ΦΥΛΟ
EN:	GENDER NEUTRAL
FR:	NON DISCRIMINATOIRE/NON SEXISTE
IT:	NEUTRO RISPETTO AL GENERE/SESSO
NL:	SEKSENEUTRAAL
PT:	NEUTRO EM TERMOS DE GÉNERO
FI:	SUKUPUOLINEUTRAALI
SV:	KÖNSNEUTRAL

Having no differential positive or negative impact for gender relations or equality between women and men.

ES:	DIFERENCIAL RETRIBUTIVO ENTRE MUJERES Y HOMBRES
DA:	UENS LØN TIL KVINDER OG MÆND
DE:	GESCHLECHTSSPEZIFISCHE LOHNUNTERSCHIEDE
EL:	ΔΙΑΦΟΡΟΠΟΙΗΣΗ ΣΤΙΣ ΑΜΟΙΒΕΣ ΤΩΝ ΔΥΟ ΦΥΛΩΝ
EN:	GENDER PAY DIFFERENTIAL
FR:	DIFFÉRENTIEL DE RÉMUNÉRATION ENTRE LES SEXES
IT:	DIFFERENZIALE RETRIBUTIVO FRA I SESSI
NL:	BELONINGSVERSCHILLEN TUSSEN VROUWEN EN MANNEN
PT:	DIFERENCIAL DE REMUNERAÇÃO ENTRE GÉNEROS
FI:	SUKUPUOLTEN VÄLISET PALKKAEROT
SV:	LÖNESKILLNADER MELLAN KVINNOR OCH MÄN

The existing difference between the earnings of men and women arising from job segregation and direct discrimination.

ES:	DIFERENCIA DE RETRIBUCIÓN ENTRE MUJERES Y HOMBRES
DA:	KØNSBETINGET LØNFORSKEL
DE:	GESCHLECHTSSPEZIFISCHES LOHNGEFÄLLE
EL:	ΑΝΟΙΓΜΑ ΜΕΤΑΞΥ ΤΩΝ ΑΜΟΙΒΩΝ ΤΩΝ ΔΥΟ ΦΥΛΩΝ
EN:	GENDER PAY GAP
FR:	ÉCART DE RÉMUNÉRATION ENTRE LES SEXES
IT:	DIVARIO RETRIBUTIVO FRA I SESSI
NL:	ONGELIJKE BELONING VAN VROUWEN EN MANNEN
PT:	FOSSO SALARIAL ENTRE GÉNEROS
FI:	SUKUPUOLTEN VÄLINEN PALKKAKUILU
SV:	LÖNEKLYFTAN MELLAN KVINNOR OCH MÄN

The gap between the average earnings of men and women.

GENDER PERSPECTIVE

ES:	PERSPECTIVA DE GÉNERO	IT:	CONSIDERAZIONE DELLA SPECIFICITÀ
DA:	KØNSPERSPEKTIV		DI GENERE
DE:	GESCHLECHTSSPEZIFISCHE PERSPEKTIVE	NL:	GENDERPERSPECTIEF
EL:	ΠΡΙΣΜΑ ΤΟΥ ΦΥΛΟΥ	PT:	PERSPECTIVA DE GÉNERO
EN:	GENDER PERSPECTIVE	FI:	SUKUPUOLINÄKÖKULMA
FR:	PERSPECTIVE DE GENRE	SV:	JÄMSTÄLLDHETSPERSPEKTIV

The consideration and attention given to the differences in any given policy area/activity.

GENDER PLANNING

ES:	PLANIFICACIÓN SENSIBLE AL GÉNERO	IT:	PROGRAMMAZIONE
DA:	LIGESTILLINGSPLANLÆGNING		SECONDO LA SPECIFICITÀ DI GENERE
DE:	GLEICHSTELLUNGSORIENTIERTER ANSATZ	NL:	GENDERPLANNING
EL:	ΣΧΕΔΙΑΣΜΟΣ ΠΟΥ ΕΝΤΑΣΣΕΙ ΤΗ ΔΙΑΣΤΑΣΗ	PT:	PLANEAMENTO EM FUNÇÃO DO GÉNERO
	ΤΟΥ ΦΥΛΟΥ	FI:	TASA-ARVOSUUNNITTELU
EN:	GENDER PLANNING	SV:	PLANERING UR ETT
FR:	PLANIFICATION INTÉGRANT		JÄMSTÄLLDHETSPERSPEKTIV
	LA DIMENSION DE GENRE		

An active approach to planning which takes gender as a key variable or criterion and which seeks to incorporate an explicit gender dimension into policy or action.

GENDER PROOFING

ES:	EVALUACIÓN GLOBAL TENIENDO EN	IT:	VERIFICA IN BASE AL GENERE
	CUENTA EL GÉNERO	NL:	EMANCIPATIETOETS
DA:	LIGESTILLINGSVURDERING	PT:	VERIFICAÇÃO DA INTEGRAÇÃO
DE:	GLEICHSTELLUNGSPRÜFUNG		DA PERSPECTIVA DO GÉNERO
EL:	ΕΠΑΛΗΘΕΥΣΗ ΩΣ ΠΡΟΣ ΤΗΝ ΕΝΤΑΞΗ ΤΗΣ	FI:	TASA-ARVONÄKÖKOHTIEN
	ΔΙΑΣΤΑΣΗΣ ΤΟΥ ΦΥΛΟΥ		HUOMIOONOTTAMISEN TARKASTUS
EN:	GENDER PROOFING	SV:	KONTROLL AV ATT
FR:	VÉRIFICATION DE LA PRISE		JÄMSTÄLLDHETSASPEKTEN BEAKTAS
	EN COMPTE DU GENRE		

A check carried out on any policy proposal to ensure that any potential gender discriminatory effects arising from that policy have been avoided and that gender equality is promoted.

G

GENDER RELATIONS

ES:	RELACIONES ENTRE HOMBRES Y MUJERES
DA:	KØNSRELATIONER
DE:	GESCHLECHTERVERHÄLTNISSE
EL:	ΣΧΕΣΕΙΣ ΦΥΛΟΥ
EN:	GENDER RELATIONS
FR:	RAPPORTS DE GENRE

IT:	RAPPORTO DI GENERE
NL:	VERHOUDINGEN TUSSEN MANNEN EN VROUWEN
PT:	RELAÇÕES DE GÉNERO
FI:	SUKUPUOLTEN VÄLINEN SUHDE
SV:	RELATIONER MELLAN KÖNEN

The relationship and unequal power distribution between women and men which characterise any specific gender system (see 'Gender contract').

GENDER RELEVANCE

ES:	PERTINENCIA CON RESPECTO AL GÉNERO
DA:	KØNSRELEVANS
DE:	GESCHLECHTSSPEZIFISCHE RELEVANZ
EL:	ΣΥΝΑΦΕΙΑ ΜΕ ΤΗ ΔΙΑΣΤΑΣΗ ΤΟΥ ΦΥΛΟΥ
EN:	GENDER RELEVANCE
FR:	PERTINENCE (AU REGARD) DU GENRE

IT:	SIGNIFICATIVO IN RELAZIONE AL GENERE
NL:	GENDERRELEVANTIE
PT:	RELEVÂNCIA EM TERMOS DO GÉNERO
FI:	MERKITYS SUKUPUOLEN KANNALTA
SV:	RELEVANS UR ETT JÄMSTÄLLDHETSPERSPEKTIV

The question of whether a particular policy or action is relevant to gender relations/equality between women and men.

GENDER ROLES

ES:	GÉNERO-ROLES ESTABLECIDOS EN FUNCIÓN DEL SEXO
DA:	KØNSROLLER
DE:	GESCHLECHTERROLLEN
EL:	ΡΟΛΟΙ ΤΩΝ ΦΥΛΩΝ
EN:	GENDER ROLES

FR:	RÔLES EN FONCTION DU GENRE
IT:	RUOLI DI GENERE
NL:	ROLPATRONEN VAN MANNEN EN VROUWEN
PT:	PAPÉIS ATRIBUÍDOS EM FUNÇÃO DO GÉNERO
FI:	SUKUPUOLIROOLIT
SV:	KÖNSROLLER

A set of prescriptions for action and behaviour allocated to women and men respectively, and inculcated and maintained as described under 'Gender contract'.

G

GENDER SENSITIVE

ES: SENSIBILIDAD CON RESPECTO AL GÉNERO
DA: KØNSOPMÆRKSOM
DE: GLEICHSTELLUNGSORIENTIERT
EL: ΕΥΑΙΣΘΗΤΟΠΟΙΗΜΕΝΟΣ/Η/Ο ΩΣ ΠΡΟΣ ΤΗ
ΔΙΑΣΤΑΣΗ ΤΟΥ ΦΥΛΟΥ
EN: GENDER SENSITIVE
FR: SENSIBLE À LA DIMENSION DE GENRE

IT: SENSIBILE ALLE SPECIFICITÀ DI GENERE
NL: GENDERBEWUST/SEKSEBEWUST/
VROUWVRIENDELIJK
PT: SENSÍVEL À DIMENSÃO DE GÉNERO
FI: SUKUPUOLISENSITIIVINEN
SV: KÖNSMEDVETEN

Addressing and taking into account the gender dimension.

GLASS CEILING

ES: TECHO DE VIDRIO
DA: GLASLOFT
DE: „GLÄSERNE DECKE"
EL: ΓΥΑΛΙΝΗ ΟΡΟΦΗ
EN: GLASS CEILING
FR: PLAFOND DE VERRE

IT: GLASS CEILING
(soffitto di cristallo, soffitto di vetro)
NL: GLAZEN PLAFOND
PT: TECTO DE VIDRO
FI: LASIKATTO
SV: GLASTAK

The invisible barrier arising from a complex set of structures in male-dominated organisations which prevents women from obtaining senior positions.

H

ES:	DESEMPLEO OCULTO	IT:	DISOCCUPAZIONE OCCULTA
DA:	SKJULT ARBEJDSLØSHED	NL:	VERBORGEN WERKLOOSHEID
DE:	VERSTECKTE ARBEITSLOSIGKEIT	PT:	DESEMPREGO OCULTO
EL:	ΑΔΗΛΗ ΑΝΕΡΓΙΑ	FI:	PIILOTYÖTTÖMYYS
EN:	HIDDEN UNEMPLOYMENT	SV:	DOLD ARBETSLÖSHET
FR:	CHÔMAGE CACHÉ/INVISIBLE		

Those who are unemployed but who do not meet the requirements of national systems of unemployment registration (requirements which may exclude women in particular).

ES:	TRABAJO A DOMICILIO	IT:	LAVORO A DOMICILIO
DA:	HJEMMEARBEJDE	NL:	THUISWERK
DE:	HEIMARBEIT	PT:	TRABALHO NO DOMICÍLIO
EL:	ΕΡΓΑΣΙΑ ΚΑΤ' ΟΙΚΟΝ	FI:	KOTONA TEHTÄVÄ TYÖ
EN:	HOMEWORK	SV:	ARBETE I HEMMET
FR:	TRAVAIL À DOMICILE		

Work carried out by a person in his or her home or in other premises of his or her choice, other than the workplace of the employer, for remuneration, which results in a product or a service as specified by the employer, irrespective of who provides the equipment, materials or other inputs used (International Labour Organisation Convention No 177).

ES:	SEGREGACIÓN HORIZONTAL	FR:	SÉGRÉGATION HORIZONTALE/SECTORIELLE
DA:	HORISONTAL KØNSOPDELING	IT:	SEGREGAZIONE ORIZZONTALE
DE:	HORIZONTALE TRENNUNG	NL:	HORIZONTALE SEGREGATIE
EL:	ΟΡΙΖΟΝΤΙΟΣ ΕΠΑΓΓΕΛΜΑΤΙΚΟΣ	PT:	SEGREGAÇÃO HORIZONTAL
	ΔΙΑΧΩΡΙΣΜΟΣ	FI:	HORISONTAALINEN ERIYTYMINEN
EN:	HORIZONTAL SEGREGATION	SV:	HORISONTELL SEGREGERING

The concentration of women and men into particular sectors and occupations (see 'Job segregation').

ES:	DERECHOS HUMANOS ESPECÍFICOS
	DE LA MUJER
DA:	KVINDERS MENNESKERETTIGHEDER
DE:	MENSCHENRECHTE DER FRAUEN
EL:	ΤΑ ΔΙΚΑΙΩΜΑΤΑ ΤΩΝ ΓΥΝΑΙΚΩΝ ΩΣ
	ΑΝΘΡΩΠΙΝΑ ΔΙΚΑΙΩΜΑΤΑ
EN:	HUMAN RIGHTS OF WOMEN

FR:	DROITS DES FEMMES INHÉRENTS
	AUX DROITS HUMAINS
IT:	DIRITTI UMANI DELLE DONNE
NL:	RECHTEN VAN DE VROUW/
	VROUWENRECHTEN
PT:	DIREITOS HUMANOS DAS MULHERES
FI:	NAISTEN IHMISOIKEUDET
SV:	KVINNORS MÄNSKLIGA RÄTTIGHETER

The rights of women and girl children as an inalienable, integral and indivisible part of universal human rights and including the concept of reproductive rights.

ILLEGAL WORK

ES:	EMPLEO ILEGAL	IT:	LAVORO CLANDESTINO
DA:	ULOVLIG BESKÆFTIGELSE	NL:	ILLEGALE ARBEID
DE:	ILLEGALE BESCHÄFTIGUNG	PT:	TRABALHO CLANDESTINO
EL:	ΠΑΡΑΝΟΜΗ ΕΡΓΑΣΙΑ	FI:	ILMAN LAILLISTA TYÖLUPAA TEHTY TYÖ
EN:	ILLEGAL WORK	SV:	ILLEGALT ARBETE
FR:	TRAVAIL CLANDESTIN		

Work performed by people who do not have a legal work permit.

INACTIVITY RATE

ES:	TASA DE INACTIVIDAD	IT:	TASSO DI INATTIVITÀ
DA:	FREKVENS AF IKKE-ERHVERVSAKTIVE	NL:	INACTIEVEN
DE:	QUOTE DER NICHTERWERBSTÄTIGEN	PT:	TAXA DE INACTIVIDADE
EL:	ΠΟΣΟΣΤΟ ΑΕΡΓΩΝ	FI:	TYÖMARKKINOIDEN ULKOPUOLELLA
EN:	INACTIVITY RATE		OLEVIEN OSUUS
FR:	TAUX D'INACTIVITÉ	SV:	ANDELEN EJ I ARBETSKRAFTEN

All persons who are not classified as employed or unemployed, expressed as a percentage of the population of working age (15 to 64).

INDIVIDUALISATION OF RIGHTS

ES:	INDIVIDUALIZACIÓN DE LOS DERECHOS	FR:	INDIVIDUALISATION DES DROITS
DA:	INDIVIDUALISERING AF RETTIGHEDER	IT:	INDIVIDUALIZZAZIONE DEI DIRITTI
DE:	INDIVIDUALISIERUNG DER ANSPRÜCHE/	NL:	INDIVIDUALISERING VAN RECHTEN
	RECHTE	PT:	INDIVIDUALIZAÇÃO DOS DIREITOS
EL:	ΕΞΑΤΟΜΙΚΕΥΣΗ ΤΩΝ ΔΙΚΑΙΩΜΑΤΩΝ	FI:	OIKEUKSIEN YKSILÖLLISTÄMINEN
EN:	INDIVIDUALISATION OF RIGHTS	SV:	INDIVIDUALISERING AV RÄTTIGHETER

Developing taxation and social security systems whereby rights accrue directly to the individual.

INDIVIDUAL RIGHTS

ES:	DERECHOS INDIVIDUALES	FR:	DROITS INDIVIDUELS/PROPRES
DA:	INDIVIDUELLE RETTIGHEDER	IT:	DIRITTI INDIVIDUALI
DE:	EIGENSTÄNDIGE ANSPRÜCHE/	NL:	INDIVIDUELE RECHTEN
	INDIVIDUELLE RECHTE	PT:	DIREITOS INDIVIDUAIS
EL:	ATOMIKA ΔΙΚΑΙΩΜΑΤΑ	FI:	YKSILÖLLISET OIKEUDET
EN:	INDIVIDUAL RIGHTS	SV:	INDIVIDUELLA RÄTTIGHETER

Rights which accrue directly to an individual (as opposed to derived rights).

INFORMAL ECONOMY/WORK

ES:	ECONOMÍA SUMERGIDA/TRABAJO SUMERGIDO	IT:	ECONOMIA SOMMERSA/
DA:	UFORMEL ØKONOMI/BESKÆFTIGELSE		LAVORO SOMMERSO
DE:	INFORMELLE WIRTSCHAFT/ARBEIT	NL:	INFORMELE SECTOR/ARBEID
EL:	ΑΝΕΠΙΣΗΜΗ ΟΙΚΟΝΟΜΙΑ/ΕΡΓΑΣΙΑ	PT:	ECONOMIA/TRABALHO INFORMAL
EN:	INFORMAL ECONOMY/WORK	FI:	EPÄVIRALLINEN TALOUS / PIMEÄ TYÖ
FR:	ÉCONOMIE INFORMELLE/TRAVAIL INFORMEL	SV:	INFORMELL EKONOMI/INFORMELLT ARBETE

Unpaid economic activities carried out for the direct benefit of the household or of relatives and friends' households on a reciprocal basis, including everyday domestic work and a great variety of self-provisioning activities and/or professional activity, whether as a sole or secondary occupation, exercised gainfully and not occasionally, yet not, or only marginally so, in fulfilment of any statutory, regulatory or contractual obligations, but excluding informal activities which are also part of the criminal economy.

INTEGRATION OF EQUAL OPPORTUNITIES/GENDER PERSPECTIVE

ES:	INTEGRACIÓN DE LA IGUALDAD DE OPORTUNIDADES/PERSPECTIVA DE GÉNERO	IT:	INTEGRAZIONE DELLE PARI OPPORTUNITÀ/ DELLA PROSPETTIVA DI GENERE
DA:	INTEGRATION AF LIGESTILLING/KØNSPERSPEKTIV	NL:	INTEGRATIE VAN GELIJKE KANSEN/ HET GENDERPERSPECTIEF IN HET BELEID
DE:	EINBEZIEHUNG DER DIMENSION DER CHANCENGLEICHHEIT/ DER GESCHLECHTSSPEZIFISCHEN PERSPEKTIVE	PT:	INTEGRAÇÃO DA IGUALDADE DE OPORTUNIDADES/PERSPECTIVA DE GÉNERO
EL:	ΕΝΤΑΞΗ ΤΗΣ ΔΙΑΣΤΑΣΗΣ ΤΗΣ ΙΣΟΤΗΤΑΣ ΕΥΚΑΙΡΙΩΝ/ΤΟΥ ΠΡΙΣΜΑΤΟΣ ΤΟΥ ΦΥΛΟΥ	FI:	TASA-ARVOULOTTUVUUDEN SISÄLLYTTÄMINEN / SUKUPUOLIULOTTU-VUUDEN SISÄLLYTTÄMINEN
EN:	INTEGRATION OF EQUAL OPPORTUNITIES/ GENDER PERSPECTIVE	SV:	INTEGRERING AV LIKA MÖJLIGHETER/ JÄMSTÄLLDHETSPERSPEKTIV
FR:	INTÉGRATION DE L'ÉGALITÉ DES CHANCES/ PERSPECTIVE DE GENRE		

See 'Gender mainstreaming'.

I

ES:	BARRERAS INVISIBLES	IT:	OSTACOLI INVISIBILI
DA:	USYNLIGE BARRIERER	NL:	VERBORGEN BELEMMERINGEN
DE:	UNSICHTBARE SCHRANKEN	PT:	BARREIRAS INVISÍVEIS
EL:	ΑΟΡΑΤΟΙ ΦΡΑΓΜΟΙ	FI:	NÄKYMÄTTÖMÄT ESTEET
EN:	INVISIBLE BARRIERS	SV:	OSYNLIGA HINDER
FR:	BARRIÈRES INVISIBLES		

Attitudes and the underlying traditional assumptions, norms and values which prevent (women's) empowerment/full participation in society.

ES:	EMPLEO/TRABAJO REMUNERADO IRREGULAR Y PRECARIO	FR:	EMPLOI IRRÉGULIER ET/OU PRÉCAIRE
		IT:	OCCUPAZIONE IRREGOLARE E PRECARIA
DA:	UREGELMÆSSIGT OG USTABILT ARBEJDE	NL:	NIET-REGULIERE EN/OF MARGINALE VORMEN VAN ARBEID
DE:	UNREGELMÄSSIGE UND/ODER UNGESCHÜTZTE BESCHÄFTIGUNGSVERHÄLTNISSE	PT:	EMPREGO OCASIONAL E/OU PRECÁRIO
EL:	ΜΗ ΚΑΝΟΝΙΚΗ Ή/ΚΑΙ ΕΠΙΣΦΑΛΗΣ ΑΠΑΣΧΟΛΗΣΗ	FI:	EPÄSÄÄNNÖLLINEN JA/TAI EPÄVARMA TYÖ
		SV:	OREGELBUNDET OCH OTRYGGT ARBETE
EN:	IRREGULAR AND/OR PRECARIOUS EMPLOYMENT		

Employment which is casual and generally not the subject of a proper contract or governed by any pay or social protection regulations.

JOB SEGREGATION/EMPLOYMENT SEGREGATION

ES:	SEGREGACIÓN EN EL EMPLEO	FR:	SÉGRÉGATION PROFESSIONNELLE/
DA:	KØNSBESTEMT ARBEJDSOPDELING		SÉGRÉGATION DES EMPLOIS
DE:	AUFTEILUNG DER BERUFSFELDER	IT:	SEGREGAZIONE OCCUPAZIONALE
EL:	ΕΠΑΓΓΕΛΜΑΤΙΚΟΣ ΔΙΑΧΩΡΙΣΜΟΣ	NL:	SEKSESEGREGATIE VAN DE ARBEIDSMARKT
EN:	JOB SEGREGATION/EMPLOYMENT	PT:	SEGREGAÇÃO NO EMPREGO/TRABALHO
	SEGREGATION	FI:	TYÖMARKKINOIDEN ERIYTYMINEN
		SV:	SEGREGERING PÅ ARBETSMARKNADEN

The concentration of women and men in different types and levels of activity and employment, with women being confined to a narrower range of occupations (horizontal segregation) than men, and to the lower grades of work (vertical segregation).

JOB SHARING

ES:	TRABAJO COMPARTIDO	IT:	CONDIVISIONE DEL LAVORO
DA:	JOBDELING	NL:	DUOBAAN
DE:	„JOB-SHARING"	PT:	PARTILHA DO TRABALHO
EL:	ΕΠΙΜΕΡΙΣΜΟΣ ΤΗΣ ΘΕΣΗΣ ΕΡΓΑΣΙΑΣ	FI:	TYÖN JAKAMINEN
EN:	JOB SHARING	SV:	ARBETSDELNING
FR:	EMPLOI PARTAGÉ		

Where a single job, and its remuneration and conditions, is shared by two (typically) or more people working to an agreed pattern or roster.

M

MAINSTREAMING

ES: «MAINSTREAMING» INTEGRACIÓN DE LA
PERSPECTIVA DE GÉNERO EN EL CONJUNTO
DE LAS POLÍTICAS / TRANSVERSALIDAD

DA: MAINSTREAMING

DE: „MAINSTREAMING"/EINBEZIEHUNG DER
DIMENSION DER CHANCENGLEICHHEIT
IN SÄMTLICHE BEREICHE DER POLITIK/
QUERSCHNITTSAUFGABE FRAUEN- UND
GLEICHSTELLUNGSPOLITIK

EL: «MAINSTREAMING» ΕΝΤΑΞΗ ΤΗΣ ΔΙΑΣΤΑΣΗΣ
ΤΟΥ ΦΥΛΟΥ/ΤΗΣ ΙΣΟΤΗΤΑΣ ΤΩΝ ΦΥΛΩΝ

EN: MAINSTREAMING

FR: *MAINSTREAMING*/INTÉGRATION
DE LA DIMENSION DE GENRE

IT: MAINSTREAMING
(integrazione della dimensione di genere)

NL: MAINSTREAMING

PT: *MAINSTREAMING*/INTEGRAÇÃO
DA IGUALDADE DE OPORTUNIDADES
EM TODAS AS POLÍTICAS

FI: "MAINSTREAMING"/LÄPÄISYPERIAATE/
VALTAVIRTAISTAMINEN

SV: "MAINSTREAMING"

See 'Gender mainstreaming'.

MATERNITY LEAVE

ES: PERMISO POR MATERNIDAD

DA: BARSELSORLOV

DE: MUTTERSCHAFTSURLAUB

EL: ΑΔΕΙΑ ΜΗΤΡΟΤΗΤΑΣ

EN: MATERNITY LEAVE

FR: CONGÉ DE MATERNITÉ

IT: CONGEDO DI MATERNITÀ

NL: ZWANGERSCHAPS- EN BEVALLINGSVERLOF

PT: LICENÇA DE MATERNIDADE

FI: ÄITIYSLOMA

SV: MAMMALEDIGHET

Leave to which a woman is entitled for a continuous period allocated
before and/or after giving birth in accordance with national legislation and
practice (Council Directive 92/85/EEC of 19 October 1992, OJ L 348,
28.11.1992).

M

MENTORING

ES:	TUTORÍA/MENTORÍA	IT:	TUTORAGGIO
DA:	MENTORORDNING	NL:	MENTORSCHAP
DE:	„MENTORING"	PT:	TUTORIA
EL:	ΚΑΘΟΔΗΓΗΣΗ	FI:	MENTOROINTI
EN:	MENTORING	SV:	MENTORSKAP
FR:	TUTORAT		

A sheltered relationship that allows learning and experimentation to take place and personal potential and new skills to flourish through a process in which one person, the mentor, supports the career and development of another, the mentee, outside the normal superior/subordinate relationship. Mentoring is increasingly used to support the personal/professional development of women.

MINIMUM WAGE

ES:	SALARIO MÍNIMO	IT:	SALARIO MINIMO
DA:	MINIMUMSLØN	NL:	MINIMUMLOON
DE:	MINDESTLOHN	PT:	SALÁRIO MÍNIMO
EL:	ΕΛΑΧΙΣΤΟΣ ΜΙΣΘΟΣ	FI:	VÄHIMMÄISPALKKA
EN:	MINIMUM WAGE	SV:	MINIMILÖN
FR:	SALAIRE MINIMAL		

A wage level defined in law or by agreement which is the lowest possible rate which an employer is permitted to pay.

O

ES: SEGREGACIÓN EN EL TRABAJO

DA: BESKÆFTIGELSESMÆSSIG KØNSOPDELING

DE: TRENNUNG IN DER BERUFSWELT

EL: ΕΠΑΓΓΕΛΜΑΤΙΚΟΣ ΔΙΑΧΩΡΙΣΜΟΣ

EN: OCCUPATIONAL SEGREGATION

FR: SÉGRÉGATION PROFESSIONNELLE

IT: SEGREGAZIONE OCCUPAZIONALE

NL: SEKSESEGREGATIE VAN DE ARBEIDSMARKT

PT: SEGREGAÇÃO PROFISSIONAL

FI: AMMATILLINEN ERIYTYMINEN

SV: YRKESMÄSSIG SEGREGERING

See 'Job segregation'.

PAID WORK

ES:	TRABAJO REMUNERADO	IT:	LAVORO RETRIBUITO
DA:	LØNNET ARBEJDE	NL:	BETAALDE ARBEID
DE:	BEZAHLTE ARBEIT	PT:	TRABALHO REMUNERADO
EL:	AMEIBOMENH EPΓAΣIA	FI:	PALKKATYÖ
EN:	PAID WORK	SV:	AVLÖNAT ARBETE
FR:	TRAVAIL RÉMUNÉRÉ		

Work which is remunerated in cash or in kind.

PARENTAL LEAVE

ES:	PERMISO PARENTAL	IT:	CONGEDO PARENTALE
DA:	FORÆLDREORLOV	NL:	OUDERSCHAPSVERLOF
DE:	ELTERNURLAUB	PT:	LICENÇA PARENTAL
EL:	ΓONIKH AΔEIA	FI:	VANHEMPAINLOMA
EN:	PARENTAL LEAVE	SV:	FÖRÄLDRALEDIGHET
FR:	CONGÉ PARENTAL		

The individual right, in principle on a non-transferable basis, to leave for all male and female workers following the birth or adoption of a child, to enable them to take care of that child (Council Directive 96/34/EC of 3 June 1996, OJ L 145, 19.6.1996).

PARITY DEMOCRACY

ES:	DEMOCRACIA PARITARIA	IT:	DEMOCRAZIA FONDATA SULLA PARITÀ
DA:	PARITETSDEMOKRATI	NL:	PARITAIRE DEMOCRATIE
DE:	PARITÄTISCHE DEMOKRATIE	PT:	DEMOCRACIA PARITÁRIA
EL:	ΔHMOKPATIA THΣ ΠΛHPOYΣ IΣOTHTAΣ	FI:	TASA-ARVOISEN OSALLISTUMISEN
EN:	PARITY DEMOCRACY		TOTEUTTAVA DEMOKRATIA
FR:	DÉMOCRATIE PARITAIRE	SV:	JÄMSTÄLLD DEMOKRATI

The concept of society as equally composed of women and men and that their full and equal enjoyment of citizenship is contingent upon their equal representation in political decision-making positions. Similar or equivalent participation rates for women and men, within a 40 to 60 range of representation, in the full democratic process is a principle of democracy.

P

ES:	TASAS DE PARTICIPACIÓN	IT:	TASSI DI PARTECIPAZIONE
DA:	DELTAGELSESFREKVENS	NL:	PARTICIPATIEGRAAD
DE:	BETEILIGUNGSQUOTEN	PT:	TAXAS DE PARTICIPAÇÃO
EL:	ΠΟΣΟΣΤΑ ΣΥΜΜΕΤΟΧΗΣ	FI:	OSALLISTUMISASTE
EN:	PARTICIPATION RATES	SV:	DELTAGARFREKVENS
FR:	TAUX DE PARTICIPATION		

The rate of participation by a defined group — for example women, men, lone parents, etc. — as a percentage of overall participation, usually in employment.

ES:	TRABAJO A TIEMPO PARCIAL	IT:	LAVORO A TEMPO PARZIALE
DA:	DELTIDSARBEJDE	NL:	DEELTIJDARBEID
DE:	TEILZEITARBEIT/TEILZEITBESCHÄFTIGUNG	PT:	EMPREGO/TRABALHO A TEMPO PARCIAL
EL:	ΕΡΓΑΣΙΑ ΜΕΡΙΚΗΣ ΑΠΑΣΧΟΛΗΣΗΣ	FI:	OSA-AIKATYÖ
EN:	PART-TIME EMPLOYMENT	SV:	DELTIDSARBETE
FR:	TRAVAIL À TEMPS PARTIEL		

Employment with working hours which are shorter than the normal or standard full-time hours.

ES:	PERMISO POR PATERNIDAD	IT:	CONGEDO DI PATERNITÀ
DA:	FÆDREORLOV	NL:	VADERSCHAPSVERLOF
DE:	VATERSCHAFTSURLAUB	PT:	LICENÇA DE PATERNIDADE
EL:	ΑΔΕΙΑ ΠΑΤΡΟΤΗΤΑΣ	FI:	ISYYSLOMA
EN:	PATERNAL LEAVE	SV:	PAPPALEDIGHET
FR:	CONGÉ DE PATERNITÉ		

Usually a fixed amount of leave for the father of a child which may be taken at the time of birth, or fixed amounts of time in any year or period of years which may be taken for reasons concerning the care responsibilities of a father for his child.

POSITIVE ACTION

ES:	ACCIÓN POSITIVA	IT:	AZIONE POSITIVA
DA:	POSITIVE FORANSTALTNINGER	NL:	POSITIEVE ACTIE
DE:	POSITIVE AKTIONEN/MASSNAHMEN	PT:	ACÇÃO POSITIVA
EL:	ΘΕΤΙΚΗ ΔΡΑΣΗ	FI:	TASA-ARVON EDISTÄMINEN /
EN:	POSITIVE ACTION		POSITIIVISET ERITYISTOIMET
FR:	ACTION POSITIVE	SV:	AKTIVA ÅTGÄRDER

Measures targeted at a particular group and intended to eliminate and prevent discrimination or to offset disadvantages arising from existing attitudes, behaviours and structures (sometimes referred to as positive discrimination).

POSITIVE DISCRIMINATION

ES:	DISCRIMINACIÓN POSITIVA	IT:	DISCRIMINAZIONE POSITIVA
DA:	POSITIV DISKRIMINERING	NL:	POSITIEVE DISCRIMINATIE
DE:	POSITIVE DISKRIMINIERUNG	PT:	DISCRIMINAÇÃO POSITIVA
EL:	ΘΕΤΙΚΗ ΔΙΑΚΡΙΣΗ	FI:	POSITIIVINEN ERITYISKOHTELU
EN:	POSITIVE DISCRIMINATION	SV:	AKTIVA ÅTGÄRDER
FR:	DISCRIMINATION POSITIVE		

See 'Positive action'.

PREFERENTIAL TREATMENT

ES:	TRATO PREFERENTE	IT:	TRATTAMENTO PREFERENZIALE
DA:	FORTRINSBEHANDLING	NL:	VOORKEURSBEHANDELING
DE:	BEVORZUGTE BEHANDLUNG	PT:	TRATAMENTO PREFERENCIAL
EL:	ΠΡΟΤΙΜΗΣΙΑΚΗ ΜΕΤΑΧΕΙΡΙΣΗ	FI:	ERITYISKOHTELU
EN:	PREFERENTIAL TREATMENT	SV:	POSITIV SÄRBEHANDLING
FR:	TRAITEMENT PRÉFÉRENTIEL		

The treatment of one individual or group of individuals in a manner which is likely to lead to better benefits, access, rights, opportunities or status than those of another individual or group of individuals. May be used positively when it implies a positive action intended to eliminate previous discriminatory practice or negatively where it is intended to maintain differentials or advantages of one individual/group of individuals over another.

Q

ES:	CUOTA		IT:	QUOTA
DA:	KVOTE		NL:	QUOTA
DE:	QUOTE		PT:	QUOTA
EL:	ΠΟΣΟΣΤΩΣΕΙΣ		FI:	KIINTIÖ
EN:	QUOTA		SV:	KVOTERING
FR:	QUOTA			

A defined proportion or share of places, seats or resources to be filled by or allocated to a specific group, generally under certain rules or criteria, and aimed at correcting a previous imbalance, usually in decision-making positions or in access to training opportunities or jobs.

R

RECOGNITION AND VALUATION OF UNPAID WORK

ES:	RECONOCIMIENTO Y VALORACIÓN DEL TRABAJO NO REMUNERADO	IT:	IDENTIFICAZIONE E VALUTAZIONE DEL LAVORO NON RETRIBUITO
DA:	ANERKENDELSE OG VÆRDIANSÆTTELSE AF ULØNNET ARBEJDE	NL:	ERKENNING EN WAARDERING VAN ONBETAALDE ARBEID
DE:	ANERKENNUNG UND WERTSCHÄTZUNG UNBEZAHLTER ARBEIT	PT:	RECONHECIMENTO E VALORIZAÇÃO DO TRABALHO NÃO REMUNERADO
EL:	ΑΝΑΓΝΩΡΙΣΗ ΚΑΙ ΑΠΟΤΙΜΗΣΗ ΤΗΣ ΜΗ ΑΜΕΙΒΟΜΕΝΗΣ ΕΡΓΑΣΙΑΣ	FI:	PALKATTOMAN TYÖN TUNNUSTAMINEN JA ARVOTTAMINEN
EN:	RECOGNITION AND VALUATION OF UNPAID WORK	SV:	ERKÄNNANDE OCH VÄRDERING AV OAVLÖNAT ARBETE
FR:	RECONNAISSANCE DU TRAVAIL NON RÉMUNÉRÉ		

Measurement, in quantitative terms, including by assessing and reflecting its value in satellite accounts, of unremunerated work that is outside the scope of national accounts (UN system of national accounts) such as domestic work, caring for children and other dependants, preparing food for the family, and community and other voluntary work.

RECONCILIATION OF WORK AND FAMILY/HOUSEHOLD LIFE

ES:	CONCILIACIÓN DEL TRABAJO Y LA VIDA FAMILIAR	IT:	CONCILIAZIONE DI VITA PROFESSIONALE E VITA FAMILIARE
DA:	BEDRE FORENING AF ARBEJDE OG FAMILIELIV	NL:	COMBINATIE VAN BEROEP EN GEZIN
DE:	VEREINBARKEIT VON BERUF UND FAMILIE	PT:	CONCILIAÇÃO DA VIDA PROFISSIONAL E FAMILIAR
EL:	ΣΥΝΔΥΑΣΜΟΣ ΕΠΑΓΓΕΛΜΑΤΙΚΟΥ ΚΑΙ ΟΙΚΟΓΕΝΕΙΑΚΟΥ ΒΙΟΥ	FI:	TYÖN JA PERHE-ELÄMÄN YHTEENSOVITTAMINEN
EN:	RECONCILIATION OF WORK AND FAMILY/HOUSEHOLD LIFE	SV:	FÖRENA ARBETE OCH FAMILJEANSVAR
FR:	CONCILIATION DU TRAVAIL ET DE LA VIE FAMILIALE		

The introduction of family and parental leave schemes, care arrangements for children and the elderly, and the development of a working environment structure and organisation which facilitates the combination of work and family/household responsibilities for women and men.

R

REFUGE

ES:	CENTRO DE ACOGIDA	IT:	CENTRO D'ACCOGLIENZA
DA:	KRISECENTER	NL:	BLIJF-VAN-MIJN-LIJFHUIS
DE:	FRAUENHAUS	PT:	REFÚGIO
EL:	ΚΕΝΤΡΟ ΚΑΚΟΠΟΙΗΜΕΝΩΝ ΓΥΝΑΙΚΩΝ	FI:	TURVAKOTI
EN:	REFUGE	SV:	MOTTAGNINGSCENTRUM
FR:	CENTRE D'ACCUEIL		

A safe place for women and children who are victims of violence in the home (shelter, crisis centre).

REGULATION OF PART-TIME WORK

ES:	REGULACIÓN DEL TRABAJO A TIEMPO PARCIAL	IT:	REGOLAMENTAZIONE DEL LAVORO PART-TIME
DA:	REGULERING AF DELTIDSARBEJDE	NL:	REGELGEVING ROND DEELTIJDARBEID
DE:	REGULIERUNG DER TEILZEITARBEIT	PT:	REGULAMENTAÇÃO DO TRABALHO A TEMPO PARCIAL
EL:	ΡΥΘΜΙΣΗ ΤΗΣ ΕΡΓΑΣΙΑΣ ΜΕΡΙΚΗΣ ΑΠΑΣΧΟΛΗΣΗΣ	FI:	OSA-AIKATYÖN SÄÄNTELY
EN:	REGULATION OF PART-TIME WORK	SV:	REGLERING AV DELTIDSARBETE
FR:	RÉGLEMENTATION DU TRAVAIL À TEMPS PARTIEL		

The introduction of rules which govern the scope and use of part-time work, aimed at preventing any form of discrimination against part-time workers, improving the quality of part-time work and facilitating the development of part-time work as a choice.

R

REPRODUCTIVE HEALTH

S:	SALUD EN MATERIA DE PROCREACIÓN/SALUD REPRODUCTIVA	FR:	SANTÉ EN MATIÈRE DE PROCRÉATION
		IT:	SALUTE RIPRODUTTIVA
A:	REPRODUKTIV SUNDHED	NL:	REPRODUCTIEVE GEZONDHEID
E:	REPRODUKTIONSGESUNDHEIT	PT:	SAÚDE REPRODUTIVA
L:	ΥΓΕΙΑ ΟΣΟΝ ΑΦΟΡΑ ΤΗΝ	FI:	LISÄÄNTYMISTERVEYS
	ΑΝΑΠΑΡΑΓΩΓΙΚΗ ΛΕΙΤΟΥΡΓΙΑ	SV:	REPRODUKTIV HÄLSA
N:	REPRODUCTIVE HEALTH		

A state of complete physical, mental and social well-being, and not merely the absence of disease or infirmity, in all matters relating to the reproductive system and to its functions and processes.

REPRODUCTIVE RIGHTS

S:	DERECHOS EN MATERIA DE PROCREACIÓN/ DERECHOS REPRODUCTIVOS	FR:	DROITS EN MATIÈRE DE PROCRÉATION
		IT:	DIRITTI IN MATERIA DI PROCREAZIONE
A:	REPRODUKTIVE RETTIGHEDER	NL:	REPRODUCTIEVE RECHTEN
E:	REPRODUKTIONSRECHTE	PT:	DIREITOS REPRODUTIVOS
L:	ΔΙΚΑΙΩΜΑΤΑ ΣΧΕΤΙΚΑ ΜΕ ΤΗΝ	FI:	LISÄÄNTYMISOIKEUDET
	ΑΝΑΠΑΡΑΓΩΓΙΚΗ ΛΕΙΤΟΥΡΓΙΑ	SV:	REPRODUKTIVA RÄTTIGHETER
N:	REPRODUCTIVE RIGHTS		

The right of any individual or couple to decide freely and responsibly on the number, spacing and timing of their children and to have the information and means to do so, and the right to attain the highest standard of sexual and reproductive health.

S

ES:	CUENTA COMPLEMENTARIA	IT:	CONTO COMPLEMENTARE
DA:	SATELLITREGNSKAB	NL:	SATELLIETREKENING
DE:	SATELLITENKONTO	PT:	CONTA SATÉLITE
EL:	ΣΥΜΠΛΗΡΩΜΑΤΙΚΟΣ ΛΟΓΑΡΙΑΣΜΟΣ	FI:	SATELLIITTITILINPITO
EN:	SATELLITE ACCOUNT	SV:	SATELLITRÄKENSKAPER
FR:	COMPTE SATELLITE		

An official account that is separate from but consistent with core nationa accounts.

ES:	SEGREGACIÓN DEL MERCADO LABORAL	IT:	SEGREGAZIONE DEL MERCATO DEL LAVORO
DA:	KØNSOPDELING AF ARBEJDSMARKEDET	NL:	SEGREGATIE VAN DE ARBEIDSMARKT
DE:	TEILUNG DES ARBEITSMARKTES	PT:	SEGREGAÇÃO DO MERCADO DE TRABALHO
EL:	ΔΙΑΧΩΡΙΣΜΟΣ ΤΗΣ ΑΓΟΡΑΣ ΕΡΓΑΣΙΑΣ	FI:	TYÖMARKKINOIDEN ERIYTYMINEN
EN:	SEGREGATION OF THE LABOUR MARKET	SV:	ARBETSMARKNADSSEGREGATION
FR:	SÉGRÉGATION DU MARCHÉ DU TRAVAIL		

See 'Job segregation'.

ES:	SEXO (en sentido biológico)	IT:	SESSO
DA:	KØN	NL:	SEKSE
DE:	(biologisches) GESCHLECHT	PT:	SEXO
EL:	ΦΥΛΟ (βιολογικό)	FI:	SUKUPUOLI (biologinen)
EN:	SEX	SV:	KÖN
FR:	SEXE		

The biological characteristics which distinguish human beings as female c male.

SEX DISAGGREGATED STATISTICS

S:	ESTADÍSTICAS DESAGREGADAS POR SEXO	IT:	DATI STATISTICI DISAGGREGATI PER SESSO
A:	KØNSSPECIFIK STATISTIK	NL:	NAAR GESLACHT UITGESPLITSTE
E:	NACH GESCHLECHT AUFGESCHLÜSSELTE		STATISTIEKEN
	STATISTIKEN	PT:	ESTATÍSTICAS REPARTIDAS POR SEXO
L:	ΣΤΑΤΙΣΤΙΚΕΣ ΚΑΤΑ ΦΥΛΟ	FI:	SUKUPUOLEN MUKAAN
N:	SEX DISAGGREGATED STATISTICS		ERIYTETYT TILASTOT
R:	STATISTIQUES VENTILÉES PAR SEXE	SV:	KÖNSUPPDELAD STATISTIK

he collection and separation of data and statistical information by sex to
nable comparative analysis (sometimes referred to as gender disaggreg-
ted statistics).

SEX DISCRIMINATION — DIRECT

S:	DISCRIMINACIÓN DIRECTA	IT:	DISCRIMINAZIONE DIRETTA
A:	KØNSDISKRIMINERING — DIREKTE	NL:	SEKSEDISCRIMINATIE, DIRECTE —
E:	DISKRIMINIERUNG, UNMITTELBARE (direkte)	PT:	DISCRIMINAÇÃO SEXUAL DIRECTA
L:	ΑΜΕΣΗ ΔΙΑΚΡΙΣΗ ΛΟΓΩ ΦΥΛΟΥ	FI:	SUKUPUOLINEN SYRJINTÄ — SUORA
N:	SEX DISCRIMINATION — DIRECT	SV:	KÖNSDISKRIMINERING — DIREKT
R:	DISCRIMINATION SEXUELLE DIRECTE		

Vhere a person is treated less favourably because of his or her sex.

SEX DISCRIMINATION — INDIRECT

S:	DISCRIMINACIÓN INDIRECTA	IT:	DISCRIMINAZIONE INDIRETTA
A:	KØNSDISKRIMINERING — INDIREKTE	NL:	SEKSEDISCRIMINATIE, INDIRECTE —
E:	DISKRIMINIERUNG, MITTELBARE (indirekte)	PT:	DISCRIMINAÇÃO SEXUAL INDIRECTA
.:	ΕΜΜΕΣΗ ΔΙΑΚΡΙΣΗ ΛΟΓΩ ΦΥΛΟΥ	FI:	SUKUPUOLINEN SYRJINTÄ — VÄLILLINEN
N:	SEX DISCRIMINATION — INDIRECT	SV:	KÖNSDISKRIMINERING INDIREKT
R:	DISCRIMINATION SEXUELLE INDIRECTE		

Vhere a law, regulation, policy or practice, which is apparently neutral, has
 disproportionate adverse impact on the members of one sex, unless the
ifference in treatment can be justified by objective factors (Council
irective 76/207/EEC of 9 February 1976, OJ L 39, 14.2.1976).

S

SEX/GENDER SYSTEM

ES:	SYSTEMA DE GÉNEROS	IT:	SISTEMA SESSUATO/FONDATO SUL GENERE
DA:	KØNSIDENTITETSSKABENDE SYSTEM	NL:	GENDERSYSTEEM
DE:	GESCHLECHTERORDNUNG	PT:	SISTEMA SOCIAL DE GÉNERO
EL:	ΣΥΣΤΗΜΑ ΔΗΜΙΟΥΡΓΙΑΣ ΤΟΥ ΦΥΛΟΥ	FI:	SUKUPUOLIJÄRJESTELMÄ
EN:	SEX/GENDER SYSTEM	SV:	GENUSSYSTEM
FR:	SYSTÈME SOCIAL DE GENRE		

A system of economic, social and political structures which sustain and reproduce distinctive gender roles and attributes of men and women (see 'Gender contract').

SEX TRADE

ES:	COMERCIO SEXUAL	FR:	COMMERCE DU SEXE
DA:	MENNESKEHANDEL I SEKSUELT ØJEMED	IT:	COMMERCIO DEL SESSO
DE:	MENSCHENHANDEL ZUM ZWECKE	NL:	SEKSHANDEL
	DER SEXUELLEN AUSBEUTUNG	PT:	COMÉRCIO DO SEXO
EL:	ΣΩΜΑΤΕΜΠΟΡΙΑ	FI:	SEKSIKAUPPA
EN:	SEX TRADE	SV:	KÖNSHANDEL

The trade in human beings, largely in women and children, for the purpose of sexual exploitation.

SEXUAL HARASSMENT

ES:	ACOSO SEXUAL	IT:	MOLESTIE SESSUALI
DA:	SEKSUEL CHIKANE	NL:	SEKSUELE INTIMIDATIE
DE:	SEXUELLE BELÄSTIGUNG	PT:	ASSÉDIO SEXUAL
EL:	ΣΕΞΟΥΑΛΙΚΗ ΠΑΡΕΝΟΧΛΗΣΗ	FI:	SUKUPUOLINEN HÄIRINTÄ / SUKUPUOLINEN
EN:	SEXUAL HARASSMENT		AHDISTELU
FR:	HARCÈLEMENT SEXUEL	SV:	SEXUELLA TRAKASSERIER

Unwanted conduct of a sexual nature or other conduct based on sex affecting the dignity of women and men (including, at work, the conduct of superiors and colleagues) (Council Resolution 90/C 157/02 of 29 May 1990, C C 157, 27.6.1990).

SEXUAL ORIENTATION

S:	INCLINACIÓN/ORIENTACIÓN SEXUAL	IT:	PROPENSIONI SESSUALI
A:	SEKSUEL ORIENTERING	NL:	SEKSUELE GEAARDHEID
E:	SEXUELLE ORIENTIERUNG	PT:	ORIENTAÇÃO SEXUAL
.:	ΣΕΞΟΥΑΛΙΚΕΣ ΠΡΟΤΙΜΗΣΕΙΣ	FI:	SUKUPUOLINEN SUUNTAUTUMINEN
N:	SEXUAL ORIENTATION	SV:	SEXUELL LÄGGNING
R:	ORIENTATION SEXUELLE		

exual preference for a person of either the same or the opposite sex
homosexuality, lesbianism, heterosexuality, bisexuality).

SEXUAL VIOLENCE

:	VIOLENCIA SEXUAL	IT:	VIOLENZA SESSUALE
A:	SEKSUEL VOLD	NL:	SEKSUEEL GEWELD
E:	SEXUELLE GEWALT	PT:	VIOLÊNCIA SEXUAL
:	ΣΕΞΟΥΑΛΙΚΗ ΒΙΑ	FI:	SUKUPUOLISTUNUT VÄKIVALTA
N:	SEXUAL VIOLENCE	SV:	SEXUELLT VÅLD
:	VIOLENCE SEXUELLE		

ee 'Gender-based violence'.

T

ES:	ENCUESTA SOBRE EL USO DEL TIEMPO	IT:	INCHIESTA SULL'IMPIEGO DEL TEMPO
DA:	TIDSANVENDELSESUNDERSØGELSE	NL:	TIJDSBESTEDINGSONDERZOEK
DE:	ZEITNUTZUNGSKONZEPT	PT:	INQUÉRITO À UTILIZAÇÃO DO TEMPO
EL:	ΜΕΛΕΤΗ ΤΗΣ ΔΙΑΘΕΣΗΣ ΤΟΥ ΧΡΟΝΟΥ	FI:	AJANKÄYTTÖTUTKIMUS
EN:	TIME-USE SURVEY	SV:	TIDSANVÄNDNINGSSTUDIE
FR:	ENQUÊTE SUR L'EMPLOI DU TEMPS		

A measurement of the use of time by women and men, particularly in relation to paid and unpaid work, market and non-market activities, and leisure and personal time.

ES:	TRATA DE SERES HUMANOS/DE MUJERES Y NIÑOS	FR:	TRAITE DES ÊTRES HUMAINS/DES FEMMES ET DES ENFANTS
DA:	MENNESKEHANDEL MED KVINDER OG BØRN	IT:	TRATTA DI ESSERI UMANI/DONNE E BAMBINI
DE:	MENSCHENHANDEL / FRAUEN- UND KINDERHANDEL	NL:	MENSENHANDEL/VROUWEN- EN KINDERHANDEL
EL:	ΣΩΜΑΤΕΜΠΟΡΙΑ ΑΝΘΡΩΠΙΝΩΝ ΟΝΤΩΝ/ ΓΥΝΑΙΚΩΝ ΚΑΙ ΠΑΙΔΙΩΝ	PT:	TRÁFICO DE SERES HUMANOS/DE MULHERES E CRIANÇAS
EN:	TRAFFICKING/TRADING IN HUMAN BEINGS/IN WOMEN AND CHILDREN	FI:	IHMISKAUPPA / NAIS- JA LAPSIKAUPPA
		V:	MÄNNISKOHANDEL/HANDEL MED KVINNOR OCH BARN

The trade in people, primarily in women and children, for the purposes of modern slavery or cheap labour or for sexual exploitation (see 'Sex trade').

UNEMPLOYMENT

S:	DESEMPLEO	IT:	DISOCCUPAZIONE
A:	ARBEJDSLØSHED	NL:	WERKLOOSHEID
E:	ARBEITSLOSIGKEIT	PT:	DESEMPREGO
L:	ANEPΓIA	FI:	TYÖTTÖMYYS
N:	UNEMPLOYMENT	SV:	ARBETSLÖSHET
R:	CHÔMAGE		

Measured against the total labour force, the number of persons who are registered as being without work, seeking work and currently available for work (European Community labour force survey).

UNPAID/UNREMUNERATED WORK

S:	TRABAJO NO REMUNERADO	IT:	LAVORO NON RETRIBUITO/
A:	ULØNNET ARBEJDE		NON REMUNERATO
E:	UNBEZAHLTE/UNENTGELTLICHE ARBEIT	NL:	ONBETAALDE ARBEID
L:	MH AMEIBOMENH EPΓAΣIA	PT:	TRABALHO NÃO REMUNERADO
N:	UNPAID/UNREMUNERATED WORK	FI:	PALKATON TYÖ
R:	TRAVAIL NON RÉMUNÉRÉ	SV:	OAVLÖNAT ARBETE

Work which carries no direct remuneration or other form of payment (see 'Recognition and valuation of unpaid work').

V

ES:	SEGREGACIÓN VERTICAL	FR:	SÉGRÉGATION VERTICALE/HIÉRARCHIQUE
DA:	VERTIKAL KØNSOPDELING	IT:	SEGREGAZIONE VERTICALE
DE:	VERTIKALE TRENNUNG	NL:	VERTICALE SEGREGATIE
EL:	ΚΑΘΕΤΟΣ ΕΠΑΓΓΕΛΜΑΤΙΚΟΣ ΔΙΑΧΩΡΙΣΜΟΣ	PT:	SEGREGAÇÃO VERTICAL
	(ΚΑΤΑ ΒΑΘΜΟ/ΚΛΙΜΑΚΙΟ ΕΥΘΥΝΗΣ)	FI:	VERTIKAALINEN ERIYTYMINEN
EN:	VERTICAL SEGREGATION	SV:	VERTIKAL SEGREGERING

The concentration of women and men in particular grades, levels of respon sibility or positions (see 'Job segregation').

ES:	FORMACIÓN PROFESIONAL	IT:	FORMAZIONE PROFESSIONALE
DA:	FAGLIG UDDANNELSE	NL:	BEROEPSOPLEIDING
DE:	BERUFS(AUS)BILDUNG	PT:	FORMAÇÃO PROFISSIONAL
EL:	ΕΠΑΓΓΕΛΜΑΤΙΚΗ ΚΑΤΑΡΤΙΣΗ	FI:	AMMATTIKOULUTUS
EN:	VOCATIONAL TRAINING	SV:	YRKESUTBILDNING
FR:	FORMATION PROFESSIONNELLE		

Any form of education which prepares for a qualification for a particula profession, trade or employment or which provides the necessary skills fc such a profession, trade or employment (Court of Justice of the Europea Communities, Case 293/83 *Gravier* [1985] ECR 593).

WIFE BATTERING/BEATING

S:	MALTRATO DE MUJERES	IT:	VIOLENZE CONIUGALI NEI CONFRONTI
DA:	HUSTRUMISHANDLING/HUSTRUVOLD		DELLA MOGLIE
DE:	MISSHANDLUNG VON FRAUEN/	NL:	VROUWENMISHANDELING
	KÖRPERLICHE GEWALT GEGEN FRAUEN	PT:	VIOLÊNCIA CONTRA AS MULHERES
L:	ΞΥΛΟΔΑΡΜΟΣ/ΚΑΚΟΠΟΙΗΣΗ ΣΥΖΥΓΟΥ		NA FAMÍLIA
N:	WIFE BATTERING/BEATING	FI:	NAISIIN KOHDISTUVA VÄKIVALTA
R:	VIOLENCE CONJUGALE/FEMMES BATTUES	SV:	HUSTRUMISSHANDEL

Violence against women by their partner (see 'Domestic violence').

WOMEN'S STUDIES/GENDER STUDIES

S:	ESTUDIOS SOBRE LA MUJER	FR:	ÉTUDES FÉMINISTES/FÉMININES/ÉTUDES
DA:	KVINDEFORSKNING/STUDIER I KØNSROLLE-		DE GENRE
	SPØRGSMÅL	IT:	STUDI SULLA DONNA/STUDI DI GENERE
DE:	FRAUENFORSCHUNG	NL:	VROUWENSTUDIES/GENDERSTUDIES
L:	ΓΥΝΑΙΚΕΙΕΣ ΣΠΟΥΔΕΣ/ΣΠΟΥΔΕΣ ΦΥΛΟΥ	PT:	ESTUDOS SOBRE AS MULHERES/DO GÉNERO
N:	WOMEN'S STUDIES/GENDER STUDIES	FI:	NAISTUTKIMUS
		SV:	KVINNOFORSKNING/GENUSFORSKNING

An academic, usually interdisciplinary approach to the analysis of women's situation and gender relations as well as the gender dimension of all other disciplines.

ropean Commission

**e hundred words for equality — A glossary of terms on equality between women
d men**

xembourg: Office for Official Publications of the European Communities

98 — 57 pp. — 14.8 x 21 cm

3N 92-828-2627-9